· ·

THE FUTURE OF
DEVELOPMENT ASSISTANCE:
COMMON POOLS AND
INTERNATIONAL PUBLIC GOODS

POLICY ESSAY NO. 25

THE FUTURE OF DEVELOPMENT ASSISTANCE: COMMON POOLS AND INTERNATIONAL PUBLIC GOODS

RAVI KANBUR AND TODD SANDLER, WITH KEVIN M. MORRISON

FOREWORD BY
NANCY BIRDSALL

DISTRIBUTED BY THE
JOHNS HOPKINS UNIVERSITY PRESS

PUBLISHED BY THE
OVERSEAS DEVELOPMENT COUNCIL
WASHINGTON, DC

Library of Congress Cataloging-In-Publication Data

Kanbur, S. M. Ravi
  The Future of Development Assistance: Common Pools and International Public Goods/ by Ravi Kanbur and Todd Sandler with Kevin M. Morrison.

       p. cm. — (ODC Policy Essay: No. 25)

    ISBN 1-56517-026-1

    1. Economic assistance. I. Sandler, Todd.   II. Morrison, Kevin M.   III. Overseas Development Council.   IV. Title.   V. Series: Policy essay: no. 25.

    HC60.K273   1999   99-37117
    338.91—dc21   CIP

Printed in the United States of America.

Publications Editor: Jacqueline Edlund-Braun
Edited by Jenepher Moseley, Scriptorium Inc.
Cover design: Design Consultants of Virginia

The views expressed in this volume are those of the authors and do not necessarily represent those of the Overseas Development Council as an organization or of its individual officers, Board, Council, advisory groups, and staff members.

Contents

Foreword

This essay is a bold attempt to change altogether the way we think about and the way we do foreign aid. It raises a deep challenge for the development community. The authors mean to be thought-provoking, and they succeed. They make a proposal about the future of foreign aid that is simple and elegant. On the one hand, their proposal is troubling—because in setting out the ideal, it necessarily abstracts from political and bureaucratic realities, and thus borders on utopian. On the other hand, their proposal notes simply what is real and true—the world is changing and the objectives and workings of foreign aid must change too.

This policy essay may seem to be written for a small audience—aficionados of "development assistance," the peculiar world of "foreign aid" transfers organized and managed by the governments of rich (donor) countries to finance activities in poor (developing) countries. But it introduces fundamental issues of much broader interest about the nature of international relations in a globalizing world. It is based on two increasingly evident (but only herein made concrete) realities. First, 50 years after the founding of the United Nations, sensible mechanisms for international cooperation on common goals are still in their infancy. Even among rich countries, sharing a relatively straightforward and apolitical goal (reduce poverty and advance democracy in poor countries), cooperation and coordination in development assistance are in all too short supply. Parochial bureaucratic and mercantile demands intrude—such that the whole of their financial and technical contributions adds up to much less than the sum of the parts. Second, that development assistance programs therefore fail to deliver is a problem for citizens of rich as well as poor countries—because we live in a world in which the rich can no longer insulate themselves from the poor, and where among the rich, traditional diplomacy and the military dominance of one country can no longer substitute for worldwide cooperation on problems that are truly global: from AIDS, to global warming, to managing global financial contagion.

So for all citizens of a global community, this essay constitutes a wake-up call: Without some radical rethinking, the development assistance and foreign aid that link rich and poor countries are at risk of growing irrelevance and eventual erosion of already fragile public support.

The proposal is elegant, and even as it aspires to the best from the bureaucrats and the politicians, it is not naïve about the way the development business currently works. The authors propose that all future development assistance aid be channeled in two ways:

- *Via a common pool mechanism.* For each eligible recipient country (with good policies, reducing corruption, etc.), rich countries would contribute to a common pool. Instead of financing individual projects or programs, rich countries would thus augment the general budget of the poor country without regard to their own parochial interests or bureaucratic needs; and

- *Via rich country spending on international public goods—programs whose benefits cannot be confined to one or another country.* Rich countries gain most when development assistance ensures that the poorest countries (the weakest links in the chain) are not, because of their poverty, the breeding ground of such global risks as new virulent disease strains and unchecked drug trafficking.

Advocates of development have bemoaned the insufficiency of aid transfers from rich to poor countries for the last three decades at least. This essay is not about that problem. It does not propose more spending. (Indeed, the authors seem to guess that a common pool approach might actually reduce spending on foreign aid for some countries for some time.) It is about making spending more effective and more relevant in a rapidly changing world (which might, in fact, enhance public support in rich countries for increasing such spending, but this is not the authors' point). The common pool approach builds on the worldwide trend to participatory democracy and the new evidence that development assistance only works where recipient countries (with reasonably good democratic governments) take charge. (The Marshall Plan worked because there was one donor, the United States, and it set up rules that ensured the Europeans would themselves take charge.) The IPG approach builds on the reality that some of today's development problems are in fact global—and beyond the purview of individual sovereign governments.

Each of these two approaches, and their implications for development assistance, could have been the topic of a separate essay. Here they are packaged together. That, as it turns out, makes sense, in part because each matters for the other, but mostly because it is together that they could, over the course of the next two or three decades, revolutionize our ideas about international cooperation and global governance.

Nancy Birdsall
Senior Associate
Carnegie Endowment for International Peace
August 1999

Acknowledgments

This essay would not have been written without the support and encouragement of Catherine Gwin, Senior Vice President of the Overseas Development Council (ODC). We thank her for her advice and guidance.

We would also like to thank Marco Ferroni, Devesh Kapur, and Nicolas van de Walle, who provided us comments that significantly improved the essay. And we particularly thank Nancy Birdsall and Joan Nelson for their detailed comments and helpful suggestions. Of course, none of these people should be held accountable for the views expressed in the essay.

Todd Sandler owes a debt of gratitude to the late Mancur Olson, who first interested him in public goods and was always a source of support.

Finally, we would like to thank Jacqueline Edlund-Braun for her editorial and production assistance.

This policy essay results from ODC's overall program of research and analysis on multilateral cooperation for development, which was made possible by the generous funding of The Ford Foundation, The John D. and Catherine T. MacArthur Foundation, the Charles Stewart Mott Foundation, and The Rockefeller Foundation. ODC's overall research program also receives funding from BankAmerica Corporation, Exxon Corporation, and Ford Motor Company. We are grateful for their support and encouragement.

Chapter 1
Introduction and
Executive Summary

As we enter the new century, the system of official development assistance that has evolved over the last 50 years faces two major challenges. The first is the disenchantment with conventional country-focused assistance, based on the perceived ineffectiveness of that assistance in achieving the objectives of development and poverty reduction. The second is the emergence of transnational problems as a major factor in global relations and in the process of development itself. These challenges in turn lead to two questions. How can the current system of aid delivery be reformed to increase its effectiveness? And what should be the relationship between development assistance and the solution of transnational problems? This policy essay addresses these two challenges through a review of current debates and a conceptual analysis of the direction in which the development assistance system should be moving. It presents a broad framework around which specific and pragmatic steps can be taken.

. . . .

AID DELIVERY AND THE "COMMON POOL" APPROACH

■   THE PROBLEMS IN THE CURRENT SYSTEM OF AID DELIVERY at the country level have been well studied, and recent reviews have highlighted and quantified the ineffectiveness of aid in promoting growth and poverty reduction.[1] Various reasons have been cited for this ineffectiveness. In addition to the well-known fact that aid has often followed political rather than development objectives,[2] these reasons include the problems of a lack of "ownership" of development projects and programs by countries receiving assistance and a lack of coordination among donors. These problems have aggravated the increasing aid dependence in the poorest countries, with policymakers spending more time in fulfilling donor requirements than in convincing their own populations of the soundness of the proposed strategies.

Some of the lack of coordination, and the myriad donor projects and programs, can be attributed to genuinely different views and perspectives on appropriate development strategies. Donors have different histories, experiences, and ideas, and these influence the projects and programs they are willing to support. At the same time, recipient countries have their own unique histories, political economies, and ideas on development strategy, which influence how they wish to act. Aid has therefore been beset by what is known as "the agency problem," the problem of one party using "sticks and carrots" to induce another party to undertake particular actions. Specific donor-funded projects, specific conditionalities on policy reform, and specific reporting requirements are all manifestations of donor attempts to resolve the agency problem. The result is a plethora of highly differentiated and diversified aid delivery systems within each country. Taken together, these dynamics have led to the current unsatisfactory system—a system which, because of its high degree of intrusiveness, creates aid dependence and undermines ownership by the country.

To the extent that this system was the product of different perspectives on development strategies, there was some hope in the late 1980s and early 1990s that a new consensus around development strategies, among donors and recipients alike, might in and of itself improve aid coordination and delivery. Such a consensus seemed likely after the fall of the Berlin Wall, with some even talking about the "end of history,"[3] referring to the triumph of free markets and outward orientation as the basis of growth and development. In economic analyses, macroeconomic stability and export orientation reigned supreme as the determinants of growth. Studies showed that when aid flowed to governments that followed sound macroeconomic policies, it did indeed contribute to growth.[4] The answer then seemed straightforward: simply target aid toward those countries that follow such sound policies. Not only would there be growth and development, but the consensus on these policies would solve the aid coordination and ownership problems as well.

Alas, at the end of the 1990s, such a consensus seems as far away as ever. And, most important, donors and recipients are likely to continue to have wide differences of opinion on the specifics of development strategy and implementation. Although there is agreement at a general level on the importance of fiscal prudence and macroeconomic stability, once one gets beyond this, into deeper social, structural, and institutional issues, consensus crumbles. And yet these issues are now viewed as equal in importance to the macroeconomic ones, especially after the social and distributional consequences of the economic crises of the late 1990s.[5] It is now understood that country-level institutions must deal with these issues with regard to the specific conditions of their country, and that there will be many differences in the approaches countries should take.[6]

The central challenge for today's conventional country-focused aid delivery system is managing divergent views on strategies for development and poverty reduction, while improving coordination, increasing ownership, and reducing aid dependence. The development community's answer to this has been "partnerships." In publications from institutions ranging from the Organization for Economic Cooperation and Development (OECD),[7] to the United Kingdom government,[8] to the World Bank,[9] partnership as a concept has received much exposure in the last two years. But partnership is not really a new idea—Lester Pearson's well-known 1969 paper was called "Partners in Development."[10] What *would* be new are specific institutional mechanisms that would form the basis of improved coordination and greater ownership.

It is argued in this policy essay that today's widely discussed emphasis on development partnerships, while welcome as an advance, falls short of providing an adequate mechanism to address the problems of coordination, ownership, and dependence. What is needed is a more radical approach in which donors really do cede control to the recipient country government, advancing their own perspective on development strategy through general dialogue with the country and with each other rather than through specific programs and projects.

This policy essay proposes a "common pool" approach to development assistance that builds on current trends and experiences but pushes them much farther. In its idealized form, it would work as follows. The recipient country would first develop its own strategy, programs, and projects, primarily in consultation with its own population but also in dialogue with donors. It would then present its plans to the donors, who would put unrestricted financing into a common pool. The common pool of development assistance, together with the government's own resources, would then finance the overall development strategy. The level of financing by each donor would depend on their own assessment both of the strategy and the program, and of the recipient country's ability to implement the strategy and effectively monitor progress and expenditures. The views based on these assessments would be made known to the country and to other donors during the dialogue leading up to the financing decision; but earmarking of this or that donor's funds to this or that item, or specific donor monitoring and control of specific projects or programs, would not be permitted.

This is of course an idealized setting, and there are many pragmatic and operational issues that need to be settled. However, the common pool approach builds on initiatives already under way, and it provides the direction in which new initiatives should move the current system. While increasing recipient ownership, it presents an institutional setting in which different views on development strategy—and therefore different donors— can coexist and better coordinate. As now, some of the donors may keep or develop their specialized focus. But this would not be in terms of financing projects and programs in particular sectors. Rather, it would be in the realm of providing specialized evaluations of the country's performance and programs, or providing specialized technical assistance to the country (but only if requested by the country within the framework of the common pool, and not earmarked).

Aid recipients following the common pool approach might experience a short-term drop-off in development assistance. However, we argue that this drop-off could be planned for, that the lower volumes would be used with greater effectiveness, and that the improved effectiveness would strengthen the argument for greater volumes of development assistance over the medium term. For donors, the common pool approach would greatly reduce the need for staff to develop, monitor, and evaluate individual projects, or to monitor adherence to conditions. Therefore, although staff would still be needed for assessment of a country's program and to dialogue with the government, we would expect the overall number of staff to decline.

. . . .

INTERNATIONAL PUBLIC GOODS, DEVELOPMENT ASSISTANCE, AND THE PRINCIPLE OF SUBSIDIARITY

■   ALONGSIDE THE CHALLENGE OF IMPROVING the effectiveness of conventional country-focused assistance, there has arisen a new challenge. A wide variety of transnational problems—for example, the spread of infectious diseases, global financial volatility, and degradation of the global environment—are increasing in magnitude as the world "globalizes" and countries become more linked to one another. Attempts to tackle these problems are examples of what are called international public goods (IPGs). IPGs are types of activities or products whose benefits spill over, wholly or partly, across two or more countries. Examples of such goods include the reduction of air pollution, basic research on vaccines, and management of global capital flows. However, because of the particular characteristics of public goods—the spillover of their benefits and the difficulty in pricing those benefits—IPGs tend to be "undersupplied." It is therefore likely that there will be, for example, too little reduction of air pollution, too little basic research on vaccines, and so on.

Correction of these undersupplies is now being discussed as a renewed rationale for development assistance.[11] IPGs can benefit both developing and developed countries. Moreover, the provision of IPGs may avoid some of the "agency" problems mentioned above, while still promoting development. In this essay, we argue that there are indeed significant interactions between IPGs and development, and that through these interactions a case can be made for financing IPGs as development assistance. For example, some problems such as the spread of AIDS are aggravated by underdevelopment and in turn affect the prospects for development. However, we argue that the case for the provision of IPGs as development assistance is more subtle and nuanced than is generally realized.

Beyond the general definition, IPGs differ enormously with respect to the nature of their undersupply, and these details have widespread implications for whether and how to support their provision through development assistance. For example, one characteristic of IPGs is the way in which access to the potential benefits of the IPG can be controlled. In some cases (like that of INTELSAT, the global satellite communications network), it is feasible to correct the global undersupply by charging beneficiaries. For development assistance, this raises the question of poorer countries' ability to pay, but this can be handled through conventional aid transfers to the country (through a common pool, if the first line of argument in this essay is followed), and there is no need to create some other means to assist the country. However, for most kinds of IPGs, this provision in the form of what are called "club goods" is not possible. For these IPGs, the transnational problem cannot be addressed through the charging of beneficiaries, and therefore some other means must be devised.

A second significant characteristic of an IPG is the manner in which individual countries' efforts aggregate into the overall supply of the IPG. For instance, for some IPGs, sometimes referred to as "weakest-link" IPGs, the country making the smallest effort to supply the good determines the overall supply of that good. Infectious disease control is an example of this, as the country with the greatest risk of the disease will determine the level of risk for its surrounding neighbors. For other IPGs, sometimes called "best-shot" IPGs, the country making the largest effort is the one that will determine the overall supply of that good. For example, in the case of basic research on vaccines, the country that puts in the largest research effort will most likely achieve the research breakthrough. These differences have crucial implications for development assistance. For best-shot IPGs, richer countries will spend their money best by producing and supplying the IPG as they desire, and poorer countries will benefit from the spillover of the IPG (such as new knowledge on vaccines). For weakest-link IPGs, rich countries will have an interest in inducing poorer countries to spend more themselves on the supply of the IPG (such as immunization programs). In these cases, however, rich countries would experience again the agency problems that have contributed to our recommending a common pool approach for conventional development assistance.

A third characteristic of IPGs is the geographical spread of the spillover. Spillovers can range from problems crossing adjacent countries to problems affecting all countries. There is a tendency in the discourse on IPGs and development assistance to attempt to solve the undersupply of IPGs with global solutions vested in global agencies. But in this essay we propose *subsidiarity* as a guiding principle for institutional arrangements correcting the undersupply of IPGs: the undersupply should be handled closest to the point where the problem occurs. This must of course be balanced against the considerations of economies of scale and scope, but subsidiarity should be the first principle for allocating institutional responsibility.

The implications of IPGs for development assistance are therefore subtle and varied. For some, correction of the undersupply can be handled through charging beneficiaries. For others, the supply of the IPGs by rich countries can help to resolve the agency problems that have plagued conventional assistance. For still others, these agency problems will continue to persist. But for all, institutional arrangements should match as closely as possible the spread of spillovers.

We expect the case for development assistance to support the provision of IPGs to strengthen in the coming years. Such arguments could of course further bolster the case for conventional assistance (delivered through the common pool) to countries addressing the undersupply of IPGs. However, we expect that donors will seek more direct ways to provide IPGs, particularly by funding those IPGs produced in donor countries, as their provision will not be beset by the agency problem. Finally, as this focus on

IPGs increases, the institutional implications of the subsidiarity principle to tackle cross-border spillovers will most likely mean a gradual shift of capacity and staff from global to regional institutions.

. . . .

PLAN OF THE ESSAY

■ THE ESSAY HAS FIVE CHAPTERS, including this introductory chapter. Chapter 2 explores the lack of consensus on development strategy and how it, combined with political pressures on both donors and recipients, has led to the problems in the current aid delivery system. Chapter 3 introduces and develops a mechanism to address these problems—the common pool approach. Chapter 4 takes up the emerging challenge of international public goods for development assistance and sets out taxonomies of the characteristics of various types of IPGs. It also highlights the importance of the principle of subsidiarity in the institutional design for supplying IPGs. Finally, Chapter 5 concludes the essay and raises some thoughts and questions about the relationship between the common pool approach and IPGs, suggesting both complementarities and tensions between them.

This policy essay is a first step in setting out the broad directions in which we believe development assistance should evolve, in light of the two challenges of the past ineffectiveness of conventional aid and the emergence of international public goods as an issue for development and development assistance. The common pool approach and the IPG framework will need to be developed further in terms of their operational implications and pragmatic implementation. But we believe that they will serve well as benchmarks and guideposts for development assistance, as the international community seeks to meet the challenges of the coming century.

Notes

[1] World Bank, *Assessing Aid: What Works, What Doesn't, and Why* (New York: Oxford University Press, 1998).

[2] Alberto Alesina and David Dollar, "Who Gives Aid to Whom and Why?" NBER Working Paper 6612 (Cambridge, MA: National Bureau of Economic Research, 1998).

[3] Francis Fukuyama, *The End of History and the Last Man* (New York: Avon Books, 1993).

[4] Craig Burnside and David Dollar, "Aid, Policies, and Growth," Policy Research Working Paper No. 1777 (Washington, DC: World Bank, Development Research Group, 1997).

[5] For example, see the "Report of G7 Finance Ministers to the Cologne Economic Summit," Cologne, Germany, June 18-20, 1999.

[6] Dani Rodrik, *The New Global Economy and Developing Countries: Making Openness Work.* Policy Essay No. 24 (Washington, DC: Overseas Development Council, 1999).

[7] OECD/DAC, *Shaping the 21st Century: The Contribution of Development Cooperation* (Paris: OECD, 1996).

[8] UK Secretary of State for International Development, "Eliminating World Poverty: A Challenge for the 21st Century," White Paper on International Development (London: The Stationery Office Ltd., 1997).

[9] World Bank Partnerships Group, "Partnership for Development: Proposed Actions for the World Bank," Discussion Paper (Washington, DC: World Bank, May 20, 1998).

[10] Lester B. Pearson, *Partners in Development: Report of the Commission on International Development* (Westport, CT: Praeger, 1969).

[11] Inge Kaul, Isabelle Grunberg, and Marc A. Stern, eds., *Global Public Goods: International Cooperation in the Twenty-First Century* (New York: Oxford University Press, 1999).

Chapter 2
The Context of
Development Assistance

Any discussion of the future of development assistance must be grounded in what we have learned both about the process of development and about assisting it over the past 50 years. To begin with, development itself is not what it used to be. When development assistance began shortly after World War II, its primary goal was spurring economic growth. But over the years, our conception of development has changed. While growth is still viewed as essential to the development process, "development" has become more focused on poverty alleviation, and its definition has widened to include such criteria as "basic human needs" (such as food, health, and education) and "capabilities" (such as the ability to partake in the life of one's community).[1]

Accordingly, the institutions of development assistance have reflected these changes. The shifting conception of development has led to increased emphasis on issues like income inequality, protection of the natural environment, and the advancement of human rights. The World Bank, for example, in its 50-year history has broadened its focus from economic growth via infrastructure development to include social sector development. Between 1950 and 1959, 61 percent of Bank lending went to infrastructure, and none of it went to social sectors. Now infrastructure represents 24 percent of Bank lending, and lending to social sectors represents 26 percent.[2] The widening of the development agenda continues even today. The World Bank is now discussing a "comprehensive development framework" that it says will enable the Bank to focus on the balance between economic, structural, social, and human aspects of development.[3]

These institutional changes have reflected not only a shifting conception of development but also a shifting consensus on the best way to pursue that development—that is, a consensus on the best development strategy. A recent study by the World Bank concluded that aid has a large effect on economic growth, poverty reduction, and social indicators when it flows into countries with "stable macro-economic environments, open trade regimes, and protected property rights, as well as efficient public bureaucracies that can deliver education, health, and other public services."[4] But this is, unfortunately, only helpful in the sense that it provides some targets for which to aim.[5] Although it is important to have come to a consensus on broad notions like the importance of macro-economic stability and education, the deeper question is *how* countries attain these things. What is the best way to create a stable macroeconomic environment? What is the best way to move to an open trade regime? How can education or health services be most effectively delivered in widely varied circumstances? The answers to these questions are the makings of development strategies.

Is there a consensus on development strategies? In short, as we will see in this chapter, there is not. Understanding that consensus has been elusive throughout the history of development assistance is essential to understanding the current way in which development assistance operates. Donors often do not agree among themselves about which policies and projects to endorse, and they often do not agree with recipients either. The system of development assistance must manage this dynamic of disagreement, and as we will see, it does not manage this disagreement very well. This is largely because of a second dynamic: the well-known tendency of both donors and recipients often to engage in development assistance on behalf of interests unrelated to development. The current way in which development assistance operates has been largely determined by the interaction of these two dynamics. As a result, assistance has unfortunately had mixed results for development.[6] We will look in the next two chapters at current thinking about how to improve development assistance. But because of the influence of these two forces, neither of which is likely to change in the near future, any reforms in the way in which aid is delivered will need to acknowledge and manage them.

· ·

THE ELUSIVE CONSENSUS ON DEVELOPMENT STRATEGY

■   TOWARD THE END OF WORLD WAR II, just before large-scale official development assistance was born, most policymakers then in office had experienced the Great Depression and therefore believed the state was needed to correct the substantial failures of the market. With regard to development, they believed that, faced with low levels of physical, human, and financial capital, it was necessary for the government to exercise control over a country's assets and economy to ensure efficient and equitable allocation of resources. Supporters of this view pointed to the Soviet Union's rapid industrialization by central state planning, and the view was exemplified by the "big-push" hypothesis.[7] India was one of many developing countries influenced by this thinking, and its first two five-year plans emphasized investment in heavy industry. Poverty, it was thought, would be taken care of by rapid, state-led industrialization.

This "consensus" was undone by major events in the world economy in the 1970s. These included the demise of the fixed exchange rate system, two oil shocks, and huge fluctuations in commodity prices, and proved too much for many countries to handle. Many viewed state interference in the economy—often exemplified by import-substitution strategies—as a primary reason why developing countries could not adjust to the changed economic environment, and state-led development began to fall out of favor. By the 1980s, one of the results of the economic turbulence and the subsequent collapse of many developing countries was a severe shortage of credit available to those countries. This shortage could only be alleviated through the resources of the World Bank and International Monetary Fund (IMF), which became even more necessary for developing countries after the debt crisis in the 1980s. The two institutions, driven primarily by the United States and other western governments, used the opportunity to influence developing countries to pursue market-led development strategies. Thus, because of both the apparent weaknesses of state-led import-substitution and the influence of the Bretton Woods Institutions, the consensus shifted from state-led development strategies to market-led ones.

The Soviet Union's collapse and the end of the Cold War seemed to provide the final evidence that the more limited a role for the state, the better.[8] However, there was strong evidence countering this. For one, there was the fact that many countries that followed the dictums of this so-called Washington Consensus did not grow.[9] In addition, some countries in Asia were doing "miraculously" seemingly because of, not despite, the state's governing of the market.[10] In the last few years, it has become clear that the right development strategy is somewhere between state-led development and the free market. The question is, "Do we know where?"

Unfortunately, no. When one goes deeper than generalities, there is little consensus now on what a development strategy should look like. To show this, let us take a closer look at two of the many issues with which every economic policymaker must deal—openness to the global economy and managing the effects of economic growth. Can a policymaker follow a "consensus" approach on either of these?

Consensus opinion about the benefits of integrating into the global economy has gone back and forth. For example, the years before World War I saw huge flows of capital and goods across borders, but with the onset of the war, countries erected barriers to capital and goods that would grow larger during the Great Depression and remain until well after World War II. The result was a massive decline in trade and capital flows. Furthermore, as mentioned above, in the years after World War II, the state-led development approach adopted by many developing countries was manifested in many of those countries in the form of import-substitution strategies, which encouraged domestic investment and industrialization by protecting domestic industries from outside competition.

Although many of the countries adhering to this strategy performed well,[11] import-substitution industrialization—and the inefficiencies it was said to cause—was largely blamed for the subsequent collapse of many countries during the turbulence of the 1970s and 1980s.[12] With the resulting shift toward a market-led approach to growth (mentioned above), many developing countries significantly lowered their barriers to capital and trade. The results have been mixed.

As Dani Rodrik, Harvard Professor and ODC Senior Advisor, argued in a recent ODC study, simply being "open" does not necessarily mean that a country will accrue the benefits of the global economy. For example, he shows that of the 25 countries with the largest increases in their ratios of exports to GDP (a common measure of openness) over the period 1975-1994, 11 averaged annual per-capita GDP growth rates of less than 1 percent. And five of them experienced *negative* growth. He notes that "although countries that grow fast tend to experience rising export-GDP ratios, the reverse is not true in general."[13] Rodrik argues that while openness has clear benefits, to maximize these benefits and minimize the hazards, countries need a strategy by which to manage openness. He maintains that such a strategy necessarily entails some government guidance of the market and possibly protection of some domestic industries.

The one region of the world that seemed to get the combination right was East Asia. From 1965 to 1990, eight countries there averaged 5.5 percent annual per-capita GDP growth, primarily driven by physical investment. Free-market proponents looked at these "miracle" countries and saw things they wanted to see: export-led growth and an adherence to economic "fundamentals."[14] But other observers pointed to the fact that almost every country that did well in East Asia also had significant government activity in the market, specifically protecting and subsidizing some industries and directing credit.[15] Much debate has surrounded the question of whether lessons from the "East Asian Miracle" are applicable to other countries. But there is little consensus except that the miracle demonstrated that developing countries could benefit greatly from the global economy. *How* they managed to benefit so much varied from country to country.

For example, Hong Kong experienced high investment rates and growth over this period using almost no barriers to capital and trade. It was able to do so primarily because its investment levels were already quite high, due to its economic and political stability in a chaotic Asia in the 1950s.[16] Countries like South Korea and Taiwan, however, faced the challenge of *raising* investment levels and employed various investment strategies to do so, openly promoting and subsidizing certain industries. Every Asian miracle country grew using a different strategy. That they all grew rapidly tells us that successful strategies for managing openness can, and perhaps *should*, vary significantly based on the varying circumstances of countries.

With the financial crisis of the late 1990s—which ironically began in this region long admired for its stable growth—it is also now painfully evident that even the Asian miracle countries did not have it exactly right. Significant questions remain about the appropriate pace and nature of integration into the world economy, including the role of capital market controls.[17] We continue to learn about the global economy and its effects, and we are far from reaching a consensus on the appropriate policies that countries should follow to thrive in the global economy.

MANAGING GROWTH

The pattern of consensus rising and falling is also apparent in the way countries have thought about how to manage the effects of economic growth—on the environment or indigenous culture, for instance. In this section, we take the issue of income distribution as an example of this struggle to deal with the societal changes that accompany growth.

In the immediate post-World War II period there was little in the way of explicit discussion of distribution in the development process. As mentioned above, the prevailing ethos was one of state-led and inward-oriented development, and the focus was on growth and industrialization, not distributional consequences. But in the mid-1950s, a number of economists began to theorize about distribution, reviving an earlier economic tradition in which development and distribution were viewed as organically linked. For example, in 1954, in a Nobel Prize-winning paper on surplus labor, Arthur Lewis put forward a model of accumulation driven by distributional forces and leading to distributional consequences.[18] And the following year, Simon Kuznets, another Nobel Prize winner, put forward his famous hypothesis that distribution worsens in the early stages of the development process and only improves much later.[19]

Within a decade, policymakers had begun to address distributional concerns. This move was due in part to evidence that the theories of Lewis and Kuznets were supported by the experiences of rapid growth economies in the 1950s and 1960s. Fishlow, for example, argued that "Kuznetsian" forces were observable in Brazil's economic take-off.[20] India worried explicitly about distribution in its third five-year plan (the official Indian poverty line was established in 1962). The World Bank began to address the issue too, in work that culminated in two major reports: 1974's *Redistribution with Growth* by Hollis Chenery and associates, and the 1980 *World Development Report.*[21] Both of these documents argued for explicit attention to distributional concerns, the latter advancing the "basic needs" doctrine of the time.

Once again, just as this consensus was forming, events took thinking in another direction. The debt crisis struck and, as mentioned above, the macroeconomic dislocations seemed to reveal major problems with the development strategies of many countries in Latin America and Africa. Many argued that the resulting shift away from state-led growth would in fact lead to growth *and* equity.[22] The incidence of poverty had generally been least in the highly protected urban sectors and greatest in those sectors that derived their returns from exports. Reforming these protected economies would therefore allow a more equitable distribution of income.

This line of thinking was seemingly supported by the experience of the East Asian miracle economies, which did not experience increases in inequality during their remarkable growth. It was argued that the outward-oriented strategy and equitable human capital investment seen in Asia were the core reasons for its equitable growth.[23] This growth contrasted with high but inequitable growth in the 1960s and 1970s in Brazil, which followed an inward-oriented path and did not invest in basic education for its population. The World Bank again took the lead in policy circles, formulating and articulating this shift in thinking in documents like the influential *World Development Reports* of 1990 and 1991,[24] and also in its work on the East Asia experience (culminating in its 1993 policy research report *The East Asian Miracle*).

And how has this consensus on export-led growth and human capital development survived the 1990s? There remains a broad consensus on the importance of investment in basic education and health. But the experiences of the 1980s and 1990s have led to new thinking about the distributional implications of market liberalization and integration into the global economy. Several arguments are advanced that acknowledge the "growth with equity" miracle of East Asia but also caution against drawing lessons too readily for the future or for other parts of the world. Some of these *caveats* include the following:

- Wood has presented evidence that, in contrast to the East Asian trade liberalizations of the 1960s and 1970s, those of Latin America in the 1980s may have increased inequalities.[25]

- The devastation of social indicators in Russia and some countries in Eastern Europe, as a result of their simultaneous liberalization and dismantling of the old safety net, has revealed the importance of domestic institutions of governance and regulation.[26]

- During the 1990s, inequality in East Asia showed signs of increasing even before the crisis.[27]

- In Africa, economic openness, even when it has led to growth and poverty reduction, has often been associated with greater inequality.[28]

- Analytical work on market-oriented reforms has also revealed more subtle patterns of distributional changes across gender[29] and across ethnic lines.[30]

Clearly much remains to be learned about income distribution; the broad consensus around how to grow equitably, which seemed within reach in the late 1980s and early 1990s, is no longer solid.[31] Policymakers will continue to wrestle with how to handle the effects of growth for many years to come.

SUMMARY

A glance at the past 50 years reveals that thinking on development strategy has constantly been in flux, influenced by historical events, economic conditions, and even ideological pressures. We have seen that, even with mainstream consensus on the importance of macroeconomic stability and human capital, significant questions continue to arise regarding the most effective way to grow and the most effective ways to manage that growth—two central issues for development. Questions also remain for other elements of development strategy, such as the detail of education or health sector reform.[32] And it is the remaining questions on overall development strategy, and the details inherent in all its aspects, that form a crucial part of the current context of development assistance.

· ·

THE POLITICS OF AID

■ DEVELOPMENT ASSISTANCE HAS, THROUGH ITS HISTORY, been driven by more than a concern for development and development strategy. It has also been driven by the political, economic, and institutional circumstances of both donors and recipients.

THE RECIPIENT

The main reason that recipients have accepted development assistance is not complex: they need the money. Despite large increases in recent years in private capital flows to developing countries overall, private capital flows to the poorest countries of the world have been and continue to be minimal.[33] The current system, unwieldy though it is, delivers the much-needed resources, and government officials have become adept at managing those resources or having the resources managed for them by donor agency personnel. Government officials derive major benefits from these resources, whether those benefits are personal or political.

This process is something of a vicious circle: the need for financial resources has been aggravated by the high ratio of aid to GDP in many countries, causing many countries to become "dependent" on aid. In other words, the more aid flows into a country, the more important that aid becomes to an economy, and the more difficult it is then for a government to refuse it. Net aid flows to African countries are often significant portions of the economy, commonly reaching 5-10 percent of GNP.[34] And there are extreme cases, such as Mozambique, where in the early 1990s foreign grants totaled around 35 percent of GNP. With the addition of debt relief and net long-term capital flows (which have been mainly in the form of multilateral loans at zero interest or near-zero interest as they are to most of the poorest countries), total foreign aid came to about 60 percent of Mozambique's GNP.[35] In cases like this, "aid dependence" seems an understatement.

THE DONOR

Donors too have reasons besides promoting development to engage in development assistance. In addition to their specific mandates and constituencies, donor agencies have been influenced by a variety of political and institutional factors that have encouraged the disbursement of aid, often regardless of the results. In fact, despite the desire of recipient governments to receive aid, most of the pressure on a country manager in a donor agency to disburse funds has historically come not from the recipient country but from internal sources. These have included:

- *Political interests.* Bilateral donor agencies (agencies representing individual countries) have almost always been closely tied to the departments of their governments involved either financially or politically in foreign relations. These departments desire the maintenance of "normal" relations, of which aid flows are often a part. In addition, these departments have pressed for the use of aid in particularly "strategic" parts of the world. For example, research has shown that being a former colony of a major donor has been a more important factor in receiving bilateral assistance than having good management.[36]

In addition, the actions of donor agencies have reflected the influence of special interest groups among their constituencies who successfully lobby their governments for (and against) certain aid projects and programs. This has been more evident in bilateral donor agencies than multilateral ones. Nevertheless, Wade's study of the way in which the environmental movement affected the actions of the World Bank shows that multilateral institutions are by no means immune.[37] Donor interests change as certain issues rise and fall in the public consciousness, with implications for whether donors continue to fund certain projects and programs in recipient countries; but donors always seek to demonstrate that they are applying money in pursuit of their constituencies' interests. This leads to pressure on donors not only to disburse funds, but also to take credit for aid programs in recipient countries, to demonstrate what they are doing for their constituencies (and the recipients).

Both of these pressures have declined somewhat with the end of the Cold War, during which the geopolitical influences on aid were most evident. It is no coincidence that government aid flows have fallen since that time, as fiscal problems in OECD countries have increased and private capital flows to developing countries have become more significant. Among the constituencies of some donors, even those groups who have supported aid for its development purposes seem to have experienced "aid fatigue" in recent years, due to the seeming ineffectiveness of aid in promoting development. It can be argued that the decline in these political pressures for aid disbursement has enabled, and even required, the reform efforts that we will discuss in the next chapter.

■ *Private sector entities.* The private sector in the donor country often has a significant stake in aid being disbursed. Companies often benefit directly from aid flows through procurement contracts with the recipient government. And if aid flows to the recipient government were lessened or suspended, the private sector in donor countries would lose out. Companies thus have an interest in seeing aid disbursed—and disbursed on time.

■ *Pressures from within the donor agency itself.* There are three main pressures from within the donor agency to disburse funds. The first pressure arises because donor funds are budgeted annually in most donor countries, and the donor agency must therefore show that it has used the funds allotted to it in the previous period. If the funds have not been used, it is difficult to ask for the same amount of funds, much less an increase, during the following replenishment period.

This pressure reinforces the second pressure, which concerns the costs of project preparation—"sunk cost." By the time projects and programs come to final decision, considerable resources have already been spent. This deters the donor agency from cutting off the project.

And finally, there is the pressure from the staff themselves. The decision not to proceed with starting a program, or to cut off payment, will almost always have significant effects on the project staff themselves. It will not only require them to find another project, but also perhaps endanger future projects on which the livelihood of that staff (often including the one making the decision to proceed with the project) depends.

. . . .

INTERACTIONS BETWEEN THE LACK OF POLICY CONSENSUS AND THE POLITICS OF AID

■   DRIVEN BY THEIR DIFFERENT POLITICAL and institutional environments, recipients and donors have become entwined in a system of development assistance despite a lack of consensus on how to pursue that development. Recipients need the financing offered by the system, and donors are driven by their own views on development strategy and a variety of political interests. There have been two main ways in which this dynamic has been manifested, one in the realm of policy and the other in the realm of development projects. With regard to policy, donors have pursued their interests by using development assistance to influence recipients to implement policies the donors think right. And with regard to projects, donors have pursued their individual institutional mandates and interests through a proliferation of their own projects. We now know that both of these approaches have had disappointing results.

INFLUENCING POLICY REFORM

From the perspective of a donor, a direct way to influence policy with development assistance money is to attach conditions of policy reform to release of aid money. If there has been one issue that has divided the development community the most in the last 15 years, it has been this issue of conditionality. Most donor governments and international institutions have adhered to the policy; many groups on the left have rallied against it, some even calling it a cause of "increasing poverty, debt, and unemployment";[38] others (including the advocacy group Oxfam) have said that conditionality itself is not the problem, but the specific conditions being assigned (exhibiting the lack of consensus on development strategy).[39]

But has conditionality, of whatever type, succeeded in achieving its goals? Although there may be numerous specific instances where conditionality helped to achieve an outcome that would otherwise not have been achieved, a recent comprehensive study concludes that "there has not been any systematic influence of aid on policy."[40] In other words, no matter which of the competing perspectives on development strategy the conditions derived from, adherence to them has been inconsistent at best.[41] Largely because of the pressures for disbursement discussed above, donors have continued to keep money flowing even when they know conditions are not often met. A 1992 report by the Operations Evaluation Department of the World Bank concluded that while the rate of recipient country compliance with conditions was very low, loan tranche release rates were very high indeed.[42] Mosley and others found a similar divergence.[43]

One consequence of the above is that aid flows have borne little relationship to policy reform. In examining the relationship between aid and an index of macroeconomic and trade policies for 56 countries, Burnside and Dollar have shown that aid has supported governments with bad policies as much as it has supported reforming governments.[44] One might argue that they observed aid going to support "bad" policies because the recipient country was about to institute reform, and the aid helped them reform. But, alas, this is also not seen. In examining 87 cases in which there was a surge in aid, and 92 cases in which there was a decline, Alesina and Dollar have shown that there is little relationship between aid changes and policy reform.[45]

The above might suggest that conditionality is irrelevant, because it bears no relation either to policy reform or whether aid flows. But while being ineffective in inducing policy reform, the process of conditionality imposes costs on the recipient. A major constraint in developing countries is the time available to a very small number of trained administrators and policymakers. Too much of this limited resource is now spent interacting with donor agencies. Killick has described how policymakers in developing countries spend so much time negotiating with donors,[46] and how the number of policy conditions for each amount of funding has been rapidly increasing.[47] These negotiations take up time that the recipient country policymakers could spend focusing on the problems of their country.

PROJECT PROLIFERATION AND THE LACK OF COORDINATION

The various political interests of donors and the lack of a consensus on development strategy have also been manifested by the creation of multiple bilateral and multilateral agencies financing projects in developing countries. Each of these agencies has its own ideas about what should take priority in the development process, and the current aid system provides them all with outlets to pursue those priorities. However, while the system accommodates this wide variety of interests on the donor side, the proliferation of projects puts an enormous burden on the recipient country trying to coordinate them. Apart from having its own priorities, each donor agency has its own requirements for how its money should be "tracked" and its own preferred ways of doing projects (even if it agrees with other donors on priorities). Like the policy conditionalities discussed above, these project conditionalities put an enormous strain on recipient government administrators and policymakers. The result is a system that is both intrusive and burdensome.

The coordination and tracking of projects occupy the time of staff in almost every department of recipient governments. For example, Wuyts gives specifics for Mozambique, where there were 405 concurrent donor-funded projects in the Ministry of Health alone.[48] Van de Walle and Johnston report that "in Tanzania, more than 2,000 projects from some 40 donors and in Ghana some 64 government or quasi-government institutions, as well as four private sector institutions, were receiving aid in the early 1990s."[49] Even an excellent bureaucracy would have trouble coordinating and accounting for so many projects.

It could be argued that this burden were bearable if the public expenditures of developing country governments were being altered toward more productive pursuits than governments would otherwise have chosen. However, evidence has shown that aid is largely fungible, meaning that resources from donors simply free up recipients' resources that can be used for other activities, perhaps ones unattractive to donors.[50] For example, if a donor is interested in funding the construction of primary schools and picks up 50 percent of the government's expenditure on this activity, the donor may be merely enabling the government to spend resources allotted for education on something else, perhaps the military.[51] This fungibility has two important implications for donor assistance, as Devarajan and Swaroop state:

> The first [implication] has to do with how donors evaluate the impact of development assistance. If funds are fungible, the traditional approach of calculating the project's rate of return will clearly not answer the question of the impact of the aid—since the aid is financing some other expenditure than the project.[52] The second implication has to do with the instruments used

by donors to deliver aid. If funds are fungible, and the recipient's public expenditure program is not satisfactory, then project lending may not be a cost-effective instrument. If the country's public expenditure program is satis-factory, the donor may as well finance a portion of this program, rather than concentrate on individual projects.[53]

THE PROBLEM OF OWNERSHIP

The time spent responding to the conditionalities, monitoring, and evaluation procedures of donors causes recipient countries to become more oriented toward donor processes and less oriented to their own. Scarce human resources are diverted away from a focus on domestic debate and building consensus about the specific needs of the developing country. Ironically, if there is a consensus emerging about development strategy, it is that such strategies should be determined to a large degree by the specific conditions in any given country—including, for example, resource base and initial levels of investment and human capital.[54] Recipient governments should be paying attention to the constantly shifting conditions of their own countries, not the constantly shifting priorities of donors.

This focus on the goals and needs of donors has also been cited as a reason for the failures of both the practice of conditionality and the prolifer-ation of projects. The failure to implement reform and much of the ineffec-tiveness of development projects can be traced to the fact that input from recipients (both recipient governments and citizens who are meant to "benefit" from the reform or project) has been relatively scarce in these processes. A recent essay summarizing the findings of a major collaborative research project on relations between donors and African recipients found that, "in spite of some improvements, donors still tend to dominate the project cycle and pay inadequate attention to the preferences of the govern-ment or project beneficiaries."[55]

This problem has received increased attention from donors recently, and it has come to be called the problem of recipient country "ownership." As van de Walle and Johnston write, "Recipient governments can be said to 'own' an aid activity when they believe that it empowers them and serves their interests."[56] This is crucial to the success of the aid activity, because unless the recipients truly believe in the reform or the project, it is unlikely that they will put any real effort into making it work. A sense of ownership can spur recipients to work to solve problems in the reform or project process and give their own resources to the process. It also makes it probable that the project or reform will be sustained even after the donor has lost interest. Moreover, a lack of country ownership almost ensures that if any difficulty arises in the reform or project process, the "beneficiaries" of the reform or project will not go very far out of their way to address them. With regard to policy reforms, for example, a World Bank paper recently said that "where reforms have been implemented and sustained, recipient country ownership of the reform process, not donor conditionality, has been the key."[57]

This lack of recipient ownership in the development assistance process is due to more than just the recipient country's weak leverage with donors. Even if the system was changed to include more input from recipient governments, it is unclear whether that input would reflect the needs of their citizens. Many developing countries lack the analytical capacity to identify effectively their own priorities and projects that need funding, and they are therefore often unable to assert needs to donors. Furthermore, even if central governments have that capacity, they often do not encourage ownership of the development process on the part of their own citizens, often the ones who most affect the success of the reform or project. Many developing countries lack the transparency, accountability, and public discussion that allow citizens to participate effectively in government activities. As found by the collaborative research project on Africa mentioned above, "Because they rarely encourage public debates about the use of aid resources, central administrations rarely understand the needs and priorities of local communities. Even the projects that ministry officials understand and support may not be owned by the beneficiaries themselves."[58] Simply receiving aid flows has often been more important to recipient country governments than ensuring that the aid funds projects and reforms desired by their people. This lack of ownership has meant that the money they have received has had much less benefit for ordinary citizens than it should have had.

It should be clear that conditionality and ownership are complicated processes, involving interaction between donors, recipient country governments, and recipient country populations. We are not arguing that donors should not have criteria or conditions for giving aid, but that the present mechanisms for implementing conditionality are seriously flawed. By definition, each donor will have its own perspective on development strategy and will view the best use of aid funds from this perspective. The key issue is whether it is feasible or desirable to force or induce the adoption of policies and strategies, which derive legitimately from the donor's perspective, by a government that does not believe in them or on a populace that will not support them. The evidence suggests that such attempts are not sustainable, and the attempts by different donors to impose their own different conditionalities have proved detrimental to the development process. There is no suggestion here that donors should give money unconditionally, rather that we need to devise an institutional mechanism whereby different perspectives can be accommodated more effectively than at present. This mechanism will be the focus of the next chapter.

. . . .

THE LESSONS FOR
DEVELOPMENT ASSISTANCE

■ THE DISCUSSION IN THIS CHAPTER HAS ILLUMINATED how two major dynamics have interacted in the field of development assistance. The lack of consensus on the details of development strategy has meant that donors and recipients find it difficult to agree between and among themselves on how best to pursue development. This has been true in the past, and it is not likely to change in the future: countries and agencies will most likely continue to differ on priorities and strategies in the development process. And yet internal pressures have spurred donors and recipients to engage in development assistance anyway.

The combination of these two forces has led to a problematic system of development assistance. The conditionality and project proliferation that have arisen have fallen short in advancing development goals. They have been too intrusive and burdensome on the developing country's capacity, and they have not encouraged the crucial component of recipient ownership of the development process at either the government or local level.

It is now readily acknowledged that if aid is to be more effective in advancing development, it will need to ensure more recipient country ownership of its policies, programs, and projects. But this will only be done by reforming development assistance in a way that successfully manages both wide differences of opinion between and within donor and recipient countries on development strategies and the pressures to disburse and receive aid that have driven aid flows for the last 50 years.

Notes

1 UNDP, *Human Development Report 1997* (New York: Oxford University Press, 1997).

2 Devesh Kapur, John P. Lewis, and Richard Webb, *The World Bank: Its First Half Century—Volume 1: History* (Washington, DC: The Brookings Institution, 1997), p. 6.

3 James D. Wolfensohn, "A Proposal for a Comprehensive Development Framework—A Discussion Draft" (Washington, DC: World Bank, 1999).

4 World Bank, *Assessing Aid: What Works, What Doesn't and Why* (New York: Oxford University Press, 1998), p. 14.

5 It should also be noted that the World Bank study did not end discussion on where aid is best used. See, for example, Henrik Hansen and Finn Tarp, "The Effectiveness of Foreign Aid," mimeo (University of Copenhagen, 1999).

6 See for example World Bank, *Assessing Aid: What Works, What Doesn't and Why*, pp. 1-2.

7 P. Rosenstein-Rodan, "Problems of Industrialization in Southern and Eastern Europe," *Economic Journal*, Vol. 53 (1943), pp. 202-11.

8 See, for example, Francis Fukuyama, *The End of History and the Last Man* (New York: Avon Books, 1993).

9 See, for example, Joseph Stiglitz, "Towards a New Paradigm for Development: Strategies, Policies, and Processes," paper given as Prebisch Lecture at UNCTAD, Geneva, October 19, 1998, forthcoming publication 1999.

10 See, for example, Robert Wade, *Governing the Market: Economic Theory and the Role of Government in East Asian Industrialization* (Princeton, NJ: Princeton University Press, 1991).

11 Dani Rodrik, *The New Global Economy and Developing Countries: Making Openness Work*, Policy Essay No. 24 (Washington, DC: Overseas Development Council, 1999).

12 Ian Little, Tibor Scitovsky, and Maurice Scott, *Trade and Industry in Some Developing Countries* (New York: Oxford University Press, 1970); and Bela Balassa and Associates, *The Structure of Protection in Developing Countries* (Baltimore, MD: Johns Hopkins University Press, 1971). Both cited in Rodrik, *The New Global Economy and Developing Countries*.

13 Rodrik, *The New Global Economy and Developing Countries*, p. 33.

14 World Bank, *The East Asian Miracle: Economic Growth and Public Policy* (New York: Oxford University Press, 1993).

15 For example, see Alice H. Amsden, "Like the Rest: South-East Asia's 'Late' Industrialization," *Journal of International Development*, Vol. 7, No. 5 (1995), pp. 791-99; and Joseph Stiglitz, "Some Lessons from the East Asian Miracle," *World Bank Research Observer*, Vol. 11, No. 2 (1996), pp. 1151-77.

16 Dani Rodrik, "TFPG Controversies, Institutions, and Economic Performance in East Asia," Working Paper 5914 (Cambridge MA: National Bureau of Economic Research, February 1997).

[17] See, for example, Barry Eichengreen and Michael Mussa, with Giovanni Dell'Ariccia, Enrica Detragiache, Gian Maria Milesi-Ferretti, and Andrew Tweedie, "Capital Account Liberalization: Theoretical and Practical Aspects," Occasional Paper No. 172 (Washington, DC: IMF, 1998); and Paul Krugman, "Saving Asia: It's Time to Get Radical," *Fortune*, September 7, 1998.

[18] W. Arthur Lewis, "Economic Development with Unlimited Supplies of Labor," *Manchester School of Economic and Social Studies*, Vol. 22 (1954), pp. 139-91.

[19] Simon Kuznets, "Economic Growth and Income Inequality," *American Economic Review*, Vol. 45, No. 1 (1955), pp. 1-28.

[20] A. Fishlow, "Brazilian Size Distribution of Income," *American Economic Review*, Vol. 62 (1972), pp. 391-402.

[21] Hollis Chenery et al., *Redistribution with Growth* (London: Oxford University Press, 1974); and World Bank, *World Development Report 1980* (New York: Oxford University Press, 1980).

[22] Ravi Kanbur, "Structural Adjustment, Macroeconomic Adjustment and Poverty: A Methodology for Analysis," *World Development*, Vol. 15, pp. 1515-26.

[23] World Bank, *The East Asian Miracle*.

[24] World Bank, *World Development Report 1990* and *World Development Report 1991: The Challenge of Development* (New York: Oxford University Press, 1990 and 1991, respectively).

[25] A. Wood, "Openness and Wage Inequality in Developing Countries: The Latin American Challenge to East Asian Conventional Wisdom," *The World Bank Economic Review*, Vol. 11, No. 1 (1997), pp. 33-58.

[26] Branko Milanovic, *Income, Inequality, and Poverty During the Transition from Planned to Market Economy* (Washington, DC: World Bank Regional and Sectoral Studies, 1997).

[27] V. Ahuja, B. Bidani, F. Ferreira, and M. Walton, *Everybody's Miracle? Revisiting Poverty and Inequality in East Asia* (Washington, DC: World Bank, 1997).

[28] L. Demery and L. Squire, "Macroeconomic Adjustment and Poverty in Africa: An Emerging Picture," *World Bank Research Observer*, Vol. 11, No. 1 (1996), pp. 39-59.

[29] R. Kanbur and L. Haddad, "Are Better Off Households More Unequal or Less Unequal?" *Oxford Economic Papers*, Vol. 46 (1994), pp. 445-58.

[30] G. Austin, "The Effects of Government Policy on Ethnic Distribution of Income and Wealth in Rwanda: A Review Of Published Sources," mimeo (London: London School of Economics, 1996).

[31] Ravi Kanbur and Nora Lustig, "Why Is Inequality Back on the Agenda?" draft April 26, 1999.

[32] For example, see Joan Nelson, *Reforming Health and Education: The World Bank, the Inter-American Development Bank, and Complex Institutional Change*, Policy Essay No. 26 (Washington, DC: ODC, forthcoming fall 1999).

[33] World Bank, *Global Development Finance* (Washington, DC: World Bank, 1998.)

[34] World Bank, *World Development Indicators* (Washington, DC: World Bank, 1998).

[35] Marc Wuyts, "Foreign Aid, Structural Adjustment, and Public Management: The Mozambican Experience," *Development and Change*, Vol. 27, No. 4 (October 1996), pp. 717-49.

[36] Alberto Alesina and David Dollar, "Who Gives Aid to Whom and Why?" NBER Working Paper 6612 (Cambridge, MA: National Bureau of Economic Research, 1998).

[37] Robert Wade, "Greening the Bank: The Struggle over the Environment, 1970-1995," in *The World Bank in Its First Half Century—Volume 2: Perspectives*, ed. Devesh Kapur, John P. Lewis, and Richard Webb (Washington, DC: The Brookings Institution, 1997), pp. 611-734.

[38] NGO Declaration at the UN Conference on Women (Beijing), 1995.

[39] Kevin Watkins, *The Oxfam Poverty Report* (Oxford: Oxfam, 1995).

[40] Craig Burnside and David Dollar, "Aid, Policies, and Growth," Policy Research Working Paper 1777 (Washington, DC: World Bank, Development Research Group, 1997).

[41] See Paul Mosley, Jane Harrigan, and John Toye, *Aid and Power*. Vol. 1. 2nd ed. (London: Routledge, 1995); and Paul Collier, "The Failure of Conditionality," in *Perspectives on Aid and Development*, ed. C. Gwin and J. Nelson, ODC Policy Essay No. 22 (Washington, DC: Overseas Development Council, 1997).

[42] World Bank, "World Bank Structural and Sectoral Adjustment Operations: The Second OED Review," Operations Evaluation Department Report No. 10870 (Washington, DC: World Bank, 1992).

[43] Mosley et. al., *Aid and Power.*

[44] Burnside and Dollar, "Aid, Policies, and Growth."

[45] Alesina and Dollar, "Who Gives Aid to Whom and Why?"

[46] T. Killick, "Conditionality and the Adjustment-Development Connection," *Pakistan Journal of Applied Economics*, Vol. XI, Nos. 1 & 2 (1995), pp. 17-36.

[47] Killick cites as an example the 1992 World Bank evaluation, which showed that the average number of conditions per adjustment loan increased from 39 between 1980-88 to 56 between 1989-1991. See World Bank, "World Bank Structural and Sectoral Adjustment Operations: The Second OED."

[48] Wuyts, "Foreign Aid, Structural Adjustment, and Public Management."

[49] Nicolas van de Walle and Timothy A. Johnston, *Improving Aid to Africa*, Policy Essay No. 21 (Washington, DC: ODC, 1996), citing Ernest Aryeetey, "Aid Effectiveness in Ghana" (manuscript, Overseas Development Institute, London, prepared for the Aid Effectiveness in Africa Project, Spring 1996).

[50] Tarhan Feyzioglu, Vinaya Swaroop, and Min Zhu, "A Panel Data Analysis of the Fungibility of Foreign Aid," *The World Bank Economic Review*, Vol. 12, No. 1 (1988), pp. 29-58.

[51] It should be recognized that although the financial component of a project is fungible, there may be other parts, such as project-specific technical assistance and capacity building, which are not. However, this still leaves open the question of whether project specific financing is necessary for this type of technical assistance. Moreover, the record of technical assistance leaves much to be desired. See Elliott Berg, *Rethinking Technical Cooperation: Reforms for Capacity Building in Africa* (New York: UNDP, 1993).

[52] Shantayanan Devarajan, Lyn Squire, and Sethaput Suthiwart-Narueput, "Beyond Rate of Return: Reorienting Project Analysis," *The World Bank Research Observer* (1997). Cited in the passage (see next note).

[53] Shantayanan Devarajan and Vinaya Swaroop, "The Implications of Foreign Aid Fungibility for Development Assistance," Policy Research Working Paper No. 2022 (Washington, DC: World Bank Development Research Group and Poverty Reduction and Economic Management Network, December 1998).

[54] See for example, Stiglitz, "Towards a New Paradigm for Development: Strategies, Policies, and Processes."

[55] van de Walle and Johnston, *Improving Aid to Africa*, p. 55.

[56] van de Walle and Johnston, *Improving Aid to Africa*, p. 54.

[57] World Bank Partnership Group, "Partnership for Development," p. 9. For examples of such studies, see Paul Collier, "The Failure of Conditionality," in *Perspectives on Aid and Development*; and van de Walle and Johnston, *Improving Aid to Africa*.

[58] van de Walle and Johnston, *Improving Aid to Africa*, p. 55.

Chapter 3
Improving
Country-Focused
Assistance:
Toward a Common
Pool Approach

With the importance of country "ownership" now widely accepted, donors and aid practitioners have begun to explore ways in which recipient countries and donors can work more effectively together. They are seeking ways to minimize coordination problems, while ensuring that more of the decisions and actions about strategy and expenditure are made by the recipient country.[1] Given what we know about development assistance,[2] it seems the ideal arrangement would have two components. First, it would give responsibility for formulating and implementing development strategies to the recipient countries, thereby increasing ownership and, thus, effectiveness in the implementation of the policies. And second, the arrangement would enable donors to judge the recipient's development strategy according to their own criteria. The donors could then act according to their own interests, both with regard to development and to the other interests that drive aid. But the key is that in the design of these two parts, the donor-recipient relationship must be altered into one with less donor interference in the domestic policy and project-implementation processes of the recipient government.

What would such a system look like? In this chapter, we propose a model called the "common pool" approach. It is a model that ensures country ownership, allows for differences of opinion in the development process, and addresses the problems of donor coordination. However, we acknowledge from the outset that this approach is a general vision, not a blueprint. We present it here because we feel it can serve as a useful guide for future efforts to improve development assistance.

Before we discuss the common pool, we look at two approaches to development assistance that the international community has taken recently and that we view as movements in the direction of the common pool. They are the sectorwide approach to development assistance and the "partnership" approach. We will argue that both of these initiatives have made strides in the right direction, but they will not completely solve the problems of donor coordination and recipient country ownership. We then explain how the "common pool approach" would more fully address these problems and what its adoption would mean for the actors involved in development assistance.

SECTORWIDE APPROACHES
TO DEVELOPMENT ASSISTANCE

■   DONORS HAVE IN THE 1990S BECOME INCREASINGLY attracted to
taking sectorwide approaches to country-focused development assistance.
This interest has arisen mainly for two reasons. First, donors are now well
aware that individual projects—even successful ones—will have a limited
impact in a poor sectoral policy environment.[3] Second, donors have realized
that the coordination problems caused by pursuing those individual projects
have meant that policymakers in developing countries have been unable to
get a clear idea of the totality of activity going on in any given sector. That
is, even if the policy environment is a good one, recipient governments may
not be able to coordinate the activities of donors.

The attempts by donors to explore the possibilities of sectorwide
approaches have incorporated much of the current thinking on the
importance of ownership.[4] At their most basic level, most of these sectorwide approaches can be described in terms of a two-step process: first,
the recipient country comes up with its strategy for the sector, and then
donors sign on to supporting the sector as a whole, not just individual
projects. The particulars of these two steps have varied, but sectorwide
approaches with these basic elements have now been implemented in
many countries around the world, including Bangladesh (health sector),
Pakistan (social sector), and Tanzania (transport sector).[5] The sectorwide
approaches have enabled recipient countries to develop the policy
environment and strategy, with the hope that this will lead to more
coordinated activities in the sector, and thereby lead to better development results.

The Zambian health sector has been held up as a prime example of
the potential of the sectorwide approach.[6] In the late 1980s and early
1990s, the health care system in Zambia was collapsing under the weight
of rapid population growth, rural-urban migration, the AIDS epidemic,
and an economy ravaged by declining commodity prices. In 1991, with the
political transformation from one-party rule to pluralist democracy, a
new government was elected and announced a wide-ranging agenda for
reform, including significant decentralization of the health sector. The
plan to reform the health sector was built on three pillars: leadership,

accountability, and partnerships. The leadership was to come from the central Ministry of Health, to ensure that the management and strategy for the health sector were both coherent. The accountability of health providers was built in to the system by making them transparent and answerable to local Health Boards that had decision making power in managerial and personnel matters. And partnerships consisting of shared workloads and responsibilities were encouraged between all actors, including: the central Ministry of Health; community representatives in the form of Health Boards and Neighborhood Health Committees; nongovernmental organizations (NGOs); and donors.

One of the most important innovations of the reforms was the relationship between the sector reform program and the international donors. With the essential elements of its health strategy developed, the Ministry of Health presented its "National Health Policies and Strategies" to the donors in 1994. In an attempt to ensure equity of services throughout the country and to aid the coherent implementation of the sector strategy, the Ministry requested that donors not directly support particular districts or provinces but instead fund the Ministry of Health centrally. Donors increasingly complied with this request for "basket funding," which provided the Ministry with more flexibility in fund allocations.[7]

With such a wide-ranging agenda for reform, it is not surprising that much of the reform effort remains unfinished as the 1990s end.[8] However, there have been some significant achievements. For example, the reforms were initially laid out in a series of corporate and strategic plans, and when additional donor funds became available in mid-1993, the Ministry made grants available to the existing 58 districts in Zambia and permitted them to plan and allocate the funds themselves. With changes in government and economic turbulence in the country, the process of reform has accelerated and decelerated often in the 1990s. However, even with the stop-and-go process, an independent review of the sector in 1997 found that "health workers are better motivated; clinics are functioning; funds are flowing to the districts; some modicum of decentralization is in place; [and] an important part of the private sector has become formally involved."[9]

The successes of the basket funding approach, though, have not attracted all donors; some worried that the funds would not be used for the purposes they intended, others were hindered by their stringent reporting requirements. As the independent review found,

Some donors have insisted on placing their own advisors in the Ministry, perhaps to reassure themselves of the proper use of the funds. Donors have also continued with projectized grants, and have attempted in recent years to support more integrated activities and fewer vertical ones. Nevertheless, despite these efforts for integrated projects, the very effect of the project itself, when felt in a district, is that of a "vertical" programme which comes in from outside the system.[10]

This Zambian case thus provides us with two lessons. First, it again enforces the importance of ownership in any reform effort. By designing their own sectoral strategy and devolving much of the responsibility in the reform process to the local level, Zambian health officials created a reform process in which Zambians felt included. That process is by no means finished or an unqualified success, but evidence seems to show that the increased ownership led to positive results.

The second lesson is that Zambia and some of its donors were able to forge a new kind of relationship that acknowledged outright the fungibility of donor funds and gave the Zambian government true ownership of the resources available to it. Although sectorwide approaches to funding have been explored and tried by a number of donor agencies, giving money to the kind of "basket" that Zambia instituted remains rare. The World Bank is an example of one donor that has tried it, by creating an operational instrument called the Sector Investment Program (SIP), in which the "project" is "the *sector*, not the actual goods and services [the program] happens to finance."[11] The SIP has six essential features:

(a) a SIP is sector-wide in scope, where a "sector" is defined as a coherent set of activities, which need to be looked at together to make a meaningful assessment, and it must cover all sector expenditures, both current and capital; (b) a SIP has to be based on a clear sector strategy and policy framework; (c) local stakeholders, meaning government, direct beneficiaries, and private sector representatives, have to be fully in charge; (d) all main donors must sign on to the approach and participate in its financing; (e) implementation arrangements should to the extent possible be common to all financiers; and (f) local capacity, rather than long term technical assistance, should be relied upon as much as possible, for the project.[12]

When these elements are in place, the Bank can view itself as a "lender of last resort" for the sector. This approach will permit other donors to choose the components of the sector strategy that suit their institutional mandates best and allow the Bank to fund the rest with confidence that the projects remaining will be productive. The Bank took this approach to the Health Sector Support Project in Ghana beginning in late 1996. The government created a five-year Program of Work that outlined all activities to be financed by funds from the government (partially with patient fees) and donors. About $650 million were thought to be needed, with government providing $360 million, other donors $240 million, and the World Bank financing the "gaps" with $50 million. [13]

However, although the SIP approach means that donors fund only projects that help to implement the strategy, it does not mean that the funds will necessarily be allocated through a sectoral pool. As the SIP study says,

> To the extent possible, all donors should accept the same arrangements for accounting, budgeting, procurement, progress reporting, etc. Preferably, these should develop through strengthening the country's own capabilities, especially with respect to the budget . . . . [But] it must be recognized that it will be a very long time before financial control and reporting systems in most of these countries will be adequate . . . , and for many donors there will be a long way to go before this can be fully entrusted to national authorities without endangering goodwill at home.[14]

The sectorwide approach therefore highlights a dilemma among donors: how to ensure full country ownership of the development process *and* be able to account for donor funds when the country has little capacity to manage them. The solution has been to let the government take control of its own sector strategy but then allow donors the ability to implement that strategy largely on their own terms. This solves some of the problems of ownership and coordination but certainly not all of them. This dilemma is evident even in sectors where the management is better than that seen throughout the rest of the country. It therefore follows that when one moves to *national* development strategies, the dilemma becomes more pronounced.

. . . .

THE PARTNERSHIP APPROACH
TO DEVELOPMENT ASSISTANCE

■   AS MENTIONED ABOVE, THE PUSH TO THINK MORE BROADLY than the project level came about partly because of a realization of the importance of the policy framework within which the project was taking place. Similar thinking has prompted a move to a perspective broader than the sector, focusing instead on a national development strategy designed and owned by the country and then supported by donors.[15] This new donor-recipient relationship has been termed, by donors, a "partnership," and it has held a significant place in their recent important policy documents. It was central in the recent United Kingdom White Paper on International Development.[16] It underlay many of the policies in the UNDP's new Programming Manual, particularly regarding the Development Assistance Framework.[17] It was also endorsed in the publication, *Shaping the 21st Century*, by the Development Cooperation Ministers and heads of aid agencies constituting the Development Assistance Committee (DAC) of the OECD.[18] Despite all the recent attention, however, it is important to remember that the concept of development partnerships is not new, having been the focus of Lester Pearson's well-known 1969 paper, "Partners in Development."[19]

The most recent partnership effort is the World Bank's, as outlined in its discussion paper, "Partnerships for Development: Proposed Actions for the World Bank."[20] The paper has been the subject of much discussion and consideration, and although many view some of its proposals with skepticism, most view it as a step in the right direction. The approach has four stages, which we review here.

Stage 1 is the assessment of the recipient country's needs. Each donor agency currently conducts its own studies to determine the needs of the recipient, usually by sector. Although sharing and learning from other donors' studies does happen occasionally, this is far from systematic. The Bank's partnership approach would change this by shifting the emphasis to the recipient country to define its own development needs through national debate and consensus building. This would be done through a consultative process including the private sector and civil society on a national and subnational level. The only donor role at this stage would be to support this consensus-building process.

Stage 2 is the design of a national development strategy based on those needs. Donors will help the country design its own strategy and action plan based on its own assessment of its needs. The consultations of Stage 1 should be the basis of this strategy, thereby allowing it to be owned by broad cross-sections of society. Donor involvement will be to the extent deemed necessary by the recipient government.

Stage 3 is the financing of the strategy designed by the country. Currently, donors usually pledge support at Consultative Groups (CGs) or

Roundtables, the main fora for aid coordination (these meetings are, however, increasingly not "pledging" sessions but instead fora for policy dialogue). At present, these meetings, and their results, are largely donor-driven. Aid coordination is, in principle (that is, in the World Bank's operational directives), the responsibility of the recipient government; but these meetings are usually chaired by a representative of the World Bank (CGs) or UNDP (Roundtables).[21] They are also often held in Paris or Geneva, far from the recipient country, thereby eliminating any possible involvement by much of the recipient country's private sector or civil society. Furthermore, donor pledges, when given, are all on different timetables and, as we have seen, driven by each donor's own priorities. This leads to a duplication of efforts in some sectors and the neglect of other sectors, and it makes organizing these pledges into a coherent strategy very difficult for the recipient country.

The Bank's proposal for this stage is to have the recipient government convene a meeting of the "Development Partners Coalition" (donors and recipient) in the recipient's capital. There will be two goals for this meeting. One will be to discuss the donors' projects in support of the national development strategy. Donors will be expected to design their own individual action plans and make their pledges, using the national development strategy as the "guiding light for each actor's actions."[22] A second goal will be to provide donors with the opportunity to coordinate their assistance strategies in "Partnership Frameworks." These frameworks would "recognize comparative advantages [of individual donors] at the country level and develop a set of modus operandi for efficient collaboration."[23]

These frameworks would be key to Stage 4, the implementation and assessment of programs and projects. As we have seen, the current situation is a chaotic one, in which all donors have their own activities with their own government contacts, reporting requirements, and goals. Even when projects are cofinanced, differences often remain about whether or not the project was a success. This would change in the Bank's approach, primarily because of the Partnership Frameworks. Donors would acknowledge that some among them are better suited for some types of assistance. They would attempt to coordinate along the lines of their comparative advantages and institute common arrangements for monitoring and assessment.

The Bank's partnership paper proposes that these agreements must be done in line with the comparative advantages of the donor agencies *in the country*, not at a global level, and that they must be done in line with the country's strategy. The Bank currently has about 25 formal cofinancing agreements with other individual donor agencies, each laying out things such as guidelines for participating in missions on cofinanced projects, and general disbursement and procurement rules governing trust fund arrangements. However, such agreements need to be done at the country level to ensure consistency with the country's strategy and capabilities. If these agreements were made at the country level they could also include mechanisms for assessing success of the shared goals; moreover, they could also attempt to harmonize the procedures and reporting requirements that are so burdensome to the country.

There are important positive aspects of the Bank's partnership approach. First and foremost, it puts the responsibility on the recipient country to assess its own needs and design its own *national* development strategy, through interaction among government, private sector, and civil society. Although its partnership approach is relatively new, the Bank cites four countries—Bolivia, Dominican Republic, El Salvador, and Ghana—that have successfully undertaken some type of process in which national development goals have been debated by society at large.[24] These types of processes are certainly necessary if the development strategy is to be owned by broad sections of society.

The Bank's partnership approach also advances a framework for how donors should appropriately interact with the country: facilitate the national discussion and then create individual plans of action that support the national strategy. However, in this approach, donors will continue to select specific projects and programs to fund. Thus the monitoring and coordination problems, which led Zambia to request donors to participate in "basket" funding of its health sector, will continue.

These problems of coordination underlie the recent proposal by the President of the World Bank, James Wolfensohn, of what he calls the Comprehensive Development Framework (CDF).[25] In this framework, which is directly in line with the Bank's partnership effort, he proposes a new management tool to help organize country-focused assistance. Wolfensohn recommends that a matrix be created with components of the recipient country's development strategy across the top and the development actors, including the country itself, along the side. The development actors would then outline exactly what they are doing in support of each element of the development strategy. This matrix would then essentially be a visual representation of the state of development assistance in any given country. The

World Bank has said it plans to attempt this in a total of 12 countries before it reassesses the approach.

The Bank's CDF is the most recent and perhaps the most widely discussed proposal for reforming the institutional mechanisms of development assistance. It is far reaching in concept, but some questions remain.

■ Although the Bank might say otherwise, there remains a question as to who exactly would draw up the matrix. This is a question not only about whether the country will be in charge of the process but which donors will help the most. There is a twofold concern that the process will be donor-driven and, more specifically, World Bank-driven.

■ In any case, the CDF again falls short of providing a means through which the burden of individual donor projects can be alleviated. Donors in the CDF, driven by their individual mandates and opinions on what should take precedence in the development process, decide the specific projects that they will fund. Although such earmarked funding would be included in the overall expenditure program, projects "picked" by donors would incur precisely the transaction costs of the individualized project preparation, evaluation, and monitoring that are likely to lead to loss of ownership by the recipients.

. . . .

THE COMMON POOL APPROACH
TO DEVELOPMENT ASSISTANCE

■ THESE APPROACHES TO DEVELOPMENT ASSISTANCE are moving in the right direction. They are moving toward a system that will ensure ownership of the development process by the developing country, preserve the ability of donors to support their own perspective on development, and minimize the problems of coordination. Knowing what we know, what might the ideal of that system look like?

First of all, like the partnership approach, it would be based on a *national* strategy, debated and agreed to by the widest possible cross-section of society. Only a national strategy would be able to address the holistic nature of development and the particular needs of the developing country, and only debate and discussion would ensure that both the strategy and its implementation will be fully owned by the country's people.

Second, while donors and recipients would dialogue throughout the strategy formulation process, with donors expressing their perspectives on the appropriate development strategies, there would not be discussions about specific sums of money from specific donors for specific projects. Such discussions would detrimentally affect the process of national consensus-building by undermining the country's sense of ownership.

Detailed revenue expenditure plans and scenarios would then be developed, most likely including costings of a range of options depending on the total resources that might become available. No aspect of government expenditures or resources would be excluded—for example, the common pool approach would subsume questions and issues of debt relief. The government would aim to manage all of its resources, including donor resources, under one budget and one set of procedures, thereby ensuring coordination and ownership of the implementation. Donors would then be presented with the plan and simply asked to transfer assistance to the central budget in an amount determined by their assessment of the strategy and the government's ability to execute it. This would resemble the process envisaged in the health sector approach for Zambia, and selectivity would be exercised through the amount of total assistance provided. Donors would commit funds for longer than a year, perhaps on a two-year or three-year basis, and these funds would not be tied to any specific conditionalities.[26] This "common pooling" of funds to the government would form the total aid resources that the country could use to finance its plan, and it would allow the government full ownership of the implementation of its plan. The common pool would be used for all normal assistance to the government from official sources.[27] This would, for example, include food aid and aid that comes from other government departments besides the donor agencies (such as, for example, in the United States, assistance from the U.S. Department of Agriculture).[28]

Under the common pool approach, there would be one development strategy—that of the country—and it would lay out all the specific projects and programs in the recipient country. Each donor's country assistance strategy would then consist of an assessment of that national development strategy and an argument for the total amount of assistance to be provided to the strategy as a whole.

Monitoring of expenditures would also be done by the recipient government, with the primary goal of reporting to its own population. There would be common reporting to all donors on the basis of information generated for domestic reporting. There could of course be dialogue on improving monitoring and reporting, but no specific conditionalities would attach to such improvements. Support could also be provided for such improvements, but only in the context of the overall expenditure plan, and only through the common pool.

The common pool approach would greatly reduce the need for specific donor coordination, even in the context of a lack of consensus on development strategy. The present cumbersome system of coordination across many donor and recipient agencies would be replaced by automatic coordination around the recipient country's development strategy. And with the ownership imbued by the strategy-setting process, the efforts to implement that strategy would be more effective.

It is important to emphasize that the common pool approach does not entail unconditional development assistance. A key feature of the approach is that donors would be able to modulate the volume of their overall assistance according to their own criteria. They could still conduct their own assessment of the recipient country's overall strategy, the consensus in the country around that strategy, and the government's ability to execute that strategy. What would not be allowed, however, is the tying of specific funds to specific projects or policy reforms, because it is this feature of the current institutional mechanism that is most problematic. It could be argued, indeed, that the common pool approach embodies a more honest, rigorous, and tougher approach to conditionality than the present fragmented approach, which the evidence suggests is not working well.

Movement to this system would have wide-ranging implications for recipients and donors, but before we address those, we need to consider the steps necessary to move toward a common pool.

. . . .

STEPS TOWARD THE COMMON POOL

■   THE COMMON POOL SYSTEM IS CLEARLY AN IDEAL. It therefore provides a direction in which future development assistance reforms should move. However, although the common pool may be implemented immediately in some developing countries, others do not as yet have the managerial and technical capacity to handle such a system. Moreover, donors will continue to feel the need to account for and monitor the use of aid resources to their own standards. Development assistance to countries should strive to develop that capacity and thereby that confidence, always with an eye toward creating the capability to run a common pool arrangement. For example, it is possible that national common pools could be built up sector by sector, as countries gradually take control of their entire national plan.

Donors can take a number of steps to help countries take control of their development process and develop capacity.[29] Donors are already taking such steps, for example, in moving some Consultative Groups and Roundtable meetings to the capital of the recipient country. These meetings should facilitate the clarity and communication necessary for donors, recipients, and citizens to work together effectively. Having these meetings in-country, as has happened for instance in Tanzania and Ethiopia, should enable more of the recipient country's government, as well as its private sector and civil society, to participate in the fora.[30] Country ownership of the process can be further encouraged if the government chairs or cochairs the meeting and provides the base documents for it. Present practice is to have such documents as Policy Framework Papers and the Public Expenditure Reviews provided by international institutions like the IMF and World Bank and therefore more owned by them than by the recipient countries.[31]

But improved donor-recipient dialogue is not all that is needed to move toward the common pool. For example, donors may not subscribe to the common pool system if recipient countries are not able to provide them with reliable data about how money is spent. This capability is in the interests of both donor and recipient governments, both of whom will need to report to their constituents. For this reason, development of recipient countries' accounting and audit capabilities should be a top priority.

One way to improve those capabilities is through technical assistance, but the record of technical assistance is not very good, particularly in countries where capacity is already weak. Analyses of technical assistance have laid the blame on many causes, chief among them that the assistance has not been demand-driven.[32] Instead, the supply of technical assistance has been driven by donors trying to monitor and ensure proper reporting on their specific projects. The assistance has also often been a form of tied aid, with much of the money going to consultants in donor countries. The result, with respect to capacity building, is that money and advice have been so closely tied together as to devalue both.

Technical assistance should therefore be one of the first areas of development assistance incorporated into the national strategy and expenditure plans of the recipient government and funded by a common pool arrangement. This will enable the technical assistance to be demand-driven, with the government free to hire the best technical assistance its money can buy. Under the common pool, there will be no connection between donor finance and the provider of the technical assistance. If there is donor dissatisfaction with the government's methods of selecting personnel for technical assistance, or even what kind of technical assistance the government requests, this can be reflected in contributions to the common pool.

Finally, greatly accelerated debt relief is necessary if the implementation of the common pool approach is to be successful. While the Group of Seven Industrialized Countries (G7) took steps to address this at the 1999 Summit in Cologne, Germany, questions remain about how the plan will be financed. It is crucial that it not only be financed, but the plan be fully implemented, if not expanded further. The debt situation in many of the poorest countries undoubtedly worsens aid effectiveness. As Kanbur argues, the problem for the heavily indebted poor countries is not so much the outflow of money to service the debt, since these countries already receive large net inflows of aid money, but rather the high transactions costs of negotiating with creditors.[33] The merry-go-round of debt reschedulings acts as a major tax on the time of the policymakers. Furthermore, the debt acts as a drag on policy reform, as people are less inclined to bear the burdens of policy reform if they feel the gains will immediately pass on to outside creditors. In fact, much of the debt can never be repaid and is basically serviced only by the aid flows. Debt relief would break this cycle and free policymakers' time and energy to build consensus on national development strategies. This is essential for the common pool approach to get off to a good start. Ultimately, debt service and debt relief would be subsumed under the common pool approach itself.

. . . .

IMPLICATIONS OF THE COMMON POOL APPROACH

■   DONORS SHOULD WORK WITH THE COUNTRY to set a target period, after which the common pool will be fully implemented. During this transition, as capabilities and country ownership are developed, aid should flow away from projects and programs with their own specific conditionalities toward a common pool arrangement. All projects ongoing at the end of that period would be allowed to run their course, and all new resources would go into the common pool. After the transition period, donors would modulate payments into the common pool commensurate with confidence in the government's strategy and system of monitoring and control.

What would this mean to both recipients and donors? How would it affect the system of development assistance?

THE DONOR

If our diagnosis of the reasons for aid ineffectiveness is correct, then the primary benefit of the common pool for the donor would be greater aid effectiveness. However, there would be some costs. It would mean giving up the practice of detailed policy conditionality, the ability to tie aid to procurement restrictions, and the ability to "track" money to a particular target. Furthermore, the nature of donor selectivity would change. Donors would still maintain selectivity in terms of the total amount contributed to each country's common pool, and their perspective on development strategy would be reflected in their dialogue with the recipient country. But the selectivity inherent in being able to pursue specific projects and programs would disappear.

These arrangements will be a problem for some donors, and possibly for the funding of development assistance in general. As the World Bank's review of Sector Investment Programs said, there are two circumstances that lead to good donor coordination: "when the government is sufficiently confident and committed to [its] approach, and when the donors are so fed up with tripping over each other that cooperation is preferable to the present situation, even with the loss of some of direct project control."[34] However, as we saw in the Zambian case, even a strong, government-owned reform program and a push by many donors for coordination do not ensure that all donors will be willing or able to participate in common funding arrangements.

If anything, this difficulty at the sector level would be increased at the national level. As we saw in the last chapter, the current system of a multitude of donor agencies pursuing their own technical and political imperatives is a reflection of both a lack of consensus on development strategy and a wide range of interests in aid flows. Many donor countries often have several bilateral programs, each of which has the support of different constituencies within the country. The same country is also almost always a member of multilateral development assistance arrangements like the multilateral banks and their concessional windows. And international public good arrangements (like the Global Environmental Facility) often see the same donors present again. This overlapping array is problematic, but it will not disappear simply by wishing it to, because in fact the mosaic represents genuinely different interests and perspectives on development and development strategies. We therefore do not believe that drastic and immediate simplification or rationalization of the bilateral and multilateral architecture of donor institutions is feasible. Rather, the common pool approach will better channel and coordinate different agencies' perspectives and mandates for the benefit of development in the recipient country.

This could, however, trigger a decline of support in donor countries for development assistance. Special interest groups will no longer be able to lobby their government to spend more money on aid projects that promote their special interests such as family planning. Instead they will only be able to lobby their governments to give money to countries that are instituting effective family planning programs. Similarly, private sector companies in donor countries will no longer be supportive of aid because of the contracts it brings them; rather, they will have to bid competitively for projects as they do now for procurement contracts resulting from multilateral development assistance.

In addition to this possibility of declining support (perhaps only in the short term), the gradual shift to the common pool approach would most likely result in a reduction in the number of aid agency personnel. For example, donor agency personnel will no longer be needed to prepare specific projects to take to their authorities, since all projects will now be part of the common pool. And they will also not be needed to monitor disbursements or projects, or to negotiate and monitor specific conditionalities.

The question of what donor agency personnel *would* do raises the question of what donor *agencies* would do in a common pool system, besides write checks. Agencies would be needed to dialogue with the recipient government and give general or technical advice if asked. And they would also be needed to assess the track record of achievement and to assess the feasibility and desirability of the government's proposed strategy and plans. All of these requirements would mean that they would need to maintain their capacity as knowledge institutions. However, in the context of a common pool arrangement, different agencies might specialize in various aspects of these roles. They might, for example, specialize in different types of assessment.

THE RECIPIENT

The benefit of the common pool approach for the recipient would be ownership of its national development strategy and therefore greater aid effectiveness, the benefits of which have been discussed sufficiently above. However, as we have seen, there are significant *caveats* that go along with this. First, formulating a national development strategy is itself an enormous and difficult task. It not only requires substantial technical knowledge to assess problems, but also, ideally, the ability to dialogue with and include the local population. The country will need to ensure that it approaches the common pool with a firm awareness of its own capabilities.

Furthermore, for many reasons the common pool approach may result, at least in the short term, in less development assistance to many developing countries. For one, as we have just seen in the preceding section, movement to the common pool approach may result in decreased development assistance overall. Another reason funds may decline is that some donors may simply not agree with some elements of the development strategy; or they may not feel that the government has the capacity to carry out some elements. Since there is no other way in the common pool approach for donors to contribute other than central budget support, they will not have any other way to transfer funds to the country. And finally, even if a donor agrees both on strategy and the capacity of the government to implement it, some donors may never be able to give up the ability to track "their" money to the projects their constituents wish to fund.

The possibility of this decline in aid will require a substantial amount of confidence on the part of recipients who adopt the approach. In the World Bank study of Sector Investment Programs, the authors said the sector-wide approach "requires a government with the will-power to say to donors: 'Here is my program in this sector: if you wish to help me implement it, you are most welcome. If you wish to do something different, I regret that you are not welcome in this sector in this country.'"[35] In the common pool approach, the government would be taking it a step further, saying essentially "Here is my national development strategy. I have discussed this with you and desire your support to help me implement it. If, however, you do not wish to support this plan through the common pool, I regret that you are not welcome to participate in development assistance in this country."

There are four main reasons why recipient governments should have the confidence to do this, if they have sufficient capacity and confidence in their national development strategy. They are as follows:

- *The recipient country should be able to see the decline in aid (if it is indeed a decline) coming.* Because of the ongoing dialogue between donors and recipients, each country should be able to predict how the policies it adopts will affect its aid flows. Therefore, if government policymakers are not able to avoid the difficulty caused by the decline of resources, they should at least be able to use policy interventions to minimize its effects. They could perhaps do this by ensuring that the pain does not fall too heavily on any one section of society.[36] In addition to this type of short-term plan, it would be advisable for the government to develop a long-term strategy for managing the inevitable shifts in aid flows. This could be done, perhaps, by devising contingency funds or other financial instruments that build up resources over time.

- *If there is any truth to the literature that has so clearly stressed the importance of ownership in determining development effectiveness, it is more important to the development of a country that its citizens subscribe to its plan than that its donors do.* Aid can help developing countries, but only if it is used effectively. And the way aid is used effectively is if a country owns its own development. In a common pool approach, government officials will have more time and leeway to interact with their own populations on development strategy, and citizens will feel included in the process and support it. This, as we have seen, is the key to reform efforts.

- *If less aid is used more productively, the impact of the drop-off in aid may not be so severe.* For example, consistency and ownership of the policy environment may have benefits for private capital inflow. There is a large literature on why the global boom in private capital flows has passed over many poor countries, particularly in Africa. Survey evidence has shown that the number one reason potential investors do not invest in Africa is the fear of policy reversal.[37] As Collier has reported, conditionality has had the perverse effect of making it difficult to know what the government was actually going to do. "The appearance of conditionality was that all reforms were done at the behest of the donors against the wishes of [recipient] governments."[38] Given the rate of recipient compliance to conditions, the agreements between donor and recipient have been, if not insignificant, at least difficult for the private sector to value when trying to predict future government policies. This was reflected in research by Dani Rodrik, who showed that international private capital flows actually decrease with the onset of a World Bank/IMF program.[39] It seems that investors see such programs as a sign of distress rather than confidence-building. With the common pool, private sector entities would have a better idea of what the government itself wants to do (and, therefore, will do), and the prospect of private capital flows may increase.

■ *If the common pool approach leads to greater aid effectiveness, then it may help to overcome the current aid fatigue in the medium term.* The drop-off in aid discussed above may therefore be mitigated to some extent.

. . . .

CONCLUSION

■ BUILDING ON THE LESSONS OF EXPERIENCE, the international community is moving toward a system of development assistance that ensures country ownership of development strategy and minimizes the intrusiveness and lack of coordination among donors, while recognizing that donors will have different perspectives on the development strategy they wish to support. In this chapter, we have shown some current examples of this movement and explained how they fall short of the "ideal"—the common pool approach. Development assistance should continue to be reformed along these lines, moving as quickly as possible to a common pool approach. We recognize that some countries are currently better able to implement this approach (and some have already moved toward doing so); while other countries will need considerable building of capacity to be able to implement the approach fully. The shift to the common pool will require adjustments on both the donor and recipient sides, and some recipient countries will need time and assistance to develop the capacity to move to the common pool. But if the common pool approach is used as a guide, the result will be more effective development assistance.

Notes

1 There is a large literature of proposals to reform development assistance. See, for example, Goran Hyden, "Reforming Foreign Aid to African Development: The Politically Autonomous Development Fund Model," *African Studies Quarterly*, Vol. 2, No. 2 (1998).

2 See Chapter 2 of this policy essay.

3 See, for example, World Bank, "Report of the World Bank Portfolio Management Task Force" (Washington, DC: World Bank, 1992).

4 See, for example, Andrew Cassels, "A Guide to Sector-Wide Approaches for Health Development: Concepts, Issues, and Working Arrangements" (Geneva: World Health Organization, 1997). This is a document the WHO co-produced with the assistance of various donor agencies. Also see Peter Harrold and Associates, "The Broad Sector Approach to Investment Lending: Sector Investment Programs," World Bank Discussion Paper 302 (Washington, DC: World Bank, 1995).

5 Harrold and Associates, "The Broad Sector Approach to Investment Lending."

6 The following discussion of the Zambia health sector comes mostly from the report of an independent review team requested by Zambia's Minister of Health to study the sector. The report was coordinated by a working group from the Ministry of Health, WHO, UNICEF, and the World Bank. It was presented in May 1997, is entitled "Comprehensive Review of the Zambian Health Reforms," and is in two volumes: the Main Report and the Technical Reports.

7 Compare this to the Mozambique case cited in Chapter 2, in which 405 concurrent donor-funded projects were going on in the Ministry of Health alone (Marc Wuyts, "Foreign Aid, Structural Adjustment, and Public Management: The Mozambican Experience," *Development and Change*, Vol. 27, No. 4 (October 1996), pp. 717-49.

8 The Health Minister appointed in early 1998 halted many of the reforms discussed in this passage.

9 "Comprehensive Review of the Zambian Health Reforms—Volume I: Main Report," p. 13.

10 "Comprehensive Review of the Zambian Health Reforms—Volume I: Main Report," p. 26.

11 Harrold and Associates, "The Broad Sector Approach to Investment Lending," p. xiv.

12 Harrold and Associates, "The Broad Sector Approach to Investment Lending," p. xi.

13 World Bank, "Ghana—Health Sector Support Program," Project Information Document, Project ID GHPA949, (Washington, DC: World Bank, 1997).

14 Harrold and Associates, "The Broad Sector Approach to Investment Lending," p. 15.

15 For more on development strategy, see Joseph Stiglitz, "Towards a New Paradigm for Development: Strategies, Policies, and Processes," paper given as Prebisch Lecture at UNCTAD, Geneva, October 19, 1998, forthcoming publication 1999; James D. Wolfensohn, "A Proposal for a Comprehensive Development Framework—A Discussion Draft" (Washington, DC: World Bank, 1999); and Joseph Stiglitz, "Participation and Development: Perspectives from the Comprehensive Development Paradigm," lecture in Seoul, Korea, February 27, 1999.

16 U.K. Secretary of State for International Development, "Eliminating World Poverty: A Challenge for the 21st Century," White Paper on International Development (London: Stationery Office Ltd., 1997).

[17] UNDP, *UNDP Programming Manual* (New York: United Nations, 1999).

[18] OECD/DAC, *Shaping the 21st Century: The Contribution of Development Cooperation* (Paris: OECD, 1996), Annex A, p. 20.

[19] Lester B. Pearson, "Partners in Development: Report of the Commission on International Development" (Westport, CT: Praeger, 1969).

[20] World Bank Partnerships Group, "Partnership for Development: Proposed Actions for the World Bank," Discussion Paper (Washington, DC: World Bank, May 20, 1998).

[21] The Inter-American Development Bank has recently chaired the Consultative Groups in some countries in Latin America.

[22] World Bank Partnerships Group, "Partnership for Development," p. 18.

[23] World Bank Partnerships Group, "Partnership for Development," p. 18.

[24] World Bank Partnerships Group, "Partnership for Development," pp. 44-45.

[25] Wolfensohn, "A Proposal for a Comprehensive Development Framework."

[26] By specific conditionalities, we mean specific sums of money being tied to specific policy reforms or specific projects being undertaken. Although the preference of donors for certain policies may have an influence on recipient country policy, the aim is to make the influence less direct.

[27] An increasing amount of development assistance is being delivered by and through private, not-for-profit organizations. Such assistance is not considered here.

[28] In the case of natural disasters and other emergencies, special arrangements may be necessary, for example, to allow donor institutions to perform relief operations themselves or to filter more funds to NGOs. However, even in these instances, they should work as closely as possible with the recipient government to make sure that the relief efforts are owned by the government.

[29] See the discussion in Ravi Kanbur, "A Framework for Thinking Through Reduced Aid Dependence," mimeo (Ithaca, NY: Cornell University, 1998). See also S. Claessens, E. Detragiache, R. Kanbur, and P. Wickham, "HIPCs' Debt Review of the Issues," *Journal of African Economies*, Vol. 6, No. 2 (1997), pp. 231-54.

[30] It can be argued that moving Consultative Groups and Roundtables to the recipient country may be detrimental since such meetings may not attract as high a level of donor representation as meetings in Paris or Geneva. But this highlights exactly what is wrong with the current system—the expectation that the major decisions are in the hands of the donors. Although transitional arrangements can and should be worked out—for example, initially holding every other meeting in the recipient country—the long-term goal should be to shift the locus of decisionmaking to the country itself.

[31] World Bank, "The Impact of Public Expenditure Reviews," Operations Evaluation Department Report 18573 (Washington, DC: World Bank, 1998).

[32] Elliott Berg, *Rethinking Technical Cooperation: Reforms for Capacity Building in Africa* (New York: UNDP, 1993).

[33] Ravi Kanbur, "Aid, Conditionality, and Debt," mimeo (Ithaca, NY: Cornell University, 1998).

[34] Harrold and Associates, "The Broad Sector Approach to Investment Lending," p. 13.

[35] Harrold and Associates, "The Broad Sector Approach to Investment Lending," pp. 12-13.

[36] For a more technical discussion of this, see Kanbur, "A Framework for Thinking Through Reduced Aid Dependence."

[37] Paul Collier, "The Failure of Conditionality," in *Perspectives on Aid and Development*, ed. Catherine Gwin and Joan Nelson, Policy Essay No. 22 (Washington, DC: Overseas Development Council, 1997), pp. 61.

[38] Collier, "The Failure of Conditionality," p. 60.

[39] Dani Rodrik, "Why Is There Multilateral Lending?" in *Annual Bank Conference on Development Economics 1995*, ed. J. M. Bruno and B. Pleskovitch (Washington, DC: World Bank, 1996), pp. 167-93.

Chapter 4
International Public Goods
and Development Assistance

During the last decade, there has been an increased awareness of cross-border spillovers in terms of vector-borne infectious diseases, acid rain, global warming, transnational terrorism, desertification, financial instabilities, insurgency-induced migrations, deteriorating labor standards, and others.[1] The world is besieged by a host of transfrontier exigencies some of which originated in developing countries, while others have greatly influenced these countries. These cross-border spillovers, which may be positive or negative, occur among developing countries, among developed countries, or between developed and developing countries. The increased prevalence of these cross-border spillovers arises from side-effects from increased market transactions, population pressures on earth's carrying capacity, unintended consequences of new technologies, the breakup of nations, and an enhanced ability to spot transfrontier spillovers. Such cross-border problems are transnational externalities in which the actions of one or more agents (e.g., multinational firms, nations, rebel groups) create costs or benefits for others, not party to the transaction. Furthermore, no automatic means exist to account for these externally imposed costs or benefits so that market prices do not adequately reflect scarcity.[2]

These uncompensated interdependencies result in too much of those activities with external costs and too little with external benefits. An important class of externalities consists of public goods, which are of particular interest for the study of development assistance, because such goods can increase human welfare by improving air quality, limiting political instabilities, augmenting communications, enhancing health, or advancing knowledge. Once a *pure* public good is provided, its benefits are available to everyone in an undiminished form.[3] If an activity (e.g., pollution) affects most recipients negatively, it is termed a "public bad," and its elimination or reduction is a public good.

The provision of public goods and/or the correction of transnational externalities can provide a new foundation for understanding and studying development assistance. This is not to say that the public good approach replaces other rationales for development assistance; rather, this new approach represents an additional reason for developed countries to want to assist developing countries. The public good approach can indicate forms of multilateral development assistance that are beneficial not only to the recipient but also to the donor. Consider the efforts of the U.S.-based Centers for Disease Control to identify new viruses and bacteria, to monitor disease outbreaks, and to coordinate research to discover a cure. These activities benefit *both* the donor and the recipient country. For the donor, such benefits can make actions to fight diseases abroad politically acceptable before they pose a threat to the donor's population. Similarly, efforts by wealthier nations to assist developing nations to substitute ozone-friendly coolants for ozone-depleting chlorofluorocarbons (CFCs) benefit donor and developing nations as ultraviolet radiation is limited worldwide. At a time when development assistance is on the decline owing to a disillusionment with past results and domestic demands for the associated resources,[4] a public good rationale can ignite a renewed interest in some kinds of development assistance activities. The dual realizations—that development assistance in the form of international public goods can help mitigate some of the negative cross-border effects stemming from the lack of development, and that this aid can improve the welfare of giver and receiver alike—can now provide a rationale for maintaining or even increasing the level of development assistance. Moreover, the mutual benefit to donors and recipients is not the only rationale behind an interest in aid in the form of international public goods. Many of these goods have wide-ranging benefits (e.g., reduced pollution, disease containment, higher labor standards) and improve the quality of life, augment productivity, and promote sustainable economic growth for all.

The primary purpose of this chapter is to present a detailed analysis of this public good approach to development assistance, while addressing a host of policy issues. It is essential that policymakers understand the nature of international public goods if they are effectively to support these goods to improve development. However, public goods are not all alike and their subtle differences—in terms of geographical spillovers, benefit characteristics, and provision properties—affect policy concerns in four ways that are explored in the course of this chapter.[5] First, there is the relationship between international public goods and development assistance, and how the provision of such goods bolsters development. Second is the way public goods are provided, whether directly by the donor or indirectly through income transfers to recipient countries. In the latter case, these international public goods can be financed through a common pool when such goods are part of the recipient country's development proposal. The third addresses the question of who should support these public goods—international agencies, private institutions, or donor countries? Coordination among diverse donors is a crucial consideration if one donor's contribution is not to crowd out or replace the public good contributions from other donors. The fourth way is to determine which institutions should be involved in providing these public goods, when support by donor countries is insufficient. This consideration leads to a principle of *subsidiarity* in which, subject to certain provisos, there should be a close match between the providing institution's jurisdictional authority and the range of benefit spillovers of the public good.[6] For example, the African Development Bank (AfDB), and not the World Bank, is the more appropriate institution to fund public goods whose range of spillover benefits is confined to Africa or its subregions. The same can be said for the Inter-American Development Bank (IDB) when the public goods' spillover range is Latin America.

At the outset, it is essential to emphasize that the public good rationale for development assistance does not eliminate the need for forms of traditional aid that alleviate poverty. In fact, some traditional development assistance takes the form of *national* public goods—e.g., schools, infrastructure—which, unlike international public goods, have few short-term international benefit spillovers, except in terms of the altruistic benefits that donors derive from making those less fortunate better off. The essential purpose of this new international public good perspective is to highlight how some forms of development assistance may abide by different considerations than traditional development assistance. With its historical country and project focus in its capital market intermediary role, the World Bank only addressed international public goods peripherally by alleviating poverty and social discontent, which could breed rebellion and conflict. Except for the World Health Organization, which drew from an earlier tradition of international cooperation on health maintenance,[7] most aid agencies were mainly concerned with country-specific development issues. The international public good approach highlights another means for providing development assistance and eliminating impediments to sustainable development. It is our contention that aid in the form of international public goods will increase as a proportion of development assistance and, in so doing, will compete with traditional aid for the same sources of funding. If, however, international public goods directly improve the well-being of the donors, then there may result an increase in development assistance.

But whatever happens to the level of this assistance, the presence of these international public goods raises free-riding considerations, because, once provided, potential donor countries receive the benefits whether or not they fund these goods. For many such public goods, there is a tendency for a small number of rich countries to do the providing, leading to a fairness concern regarding burden sharing. Changes in the distribution of income among countries globally can heighten this concern and have profound influences on which nations will provide these public goods.[8] When provision cost differs among alternative suppliers, the more efficient provider should supply relatively more of the good. In many cases, this efficiency consideration places greater burdens for providing the public good on potential donor countries than on developing countries. There is clearly a need to coordinate public good provision activities among all potential donors if crowding out (i.e., where one country's contribution to a public good merely replaces that of another country) and wasteful duplication are to be avoided. To take advantage of some international public good (e.g., a scientific discovery), a country must possess sufficient human capital and know-how, which may come with further development. Thus, development broadens the set of countries that can receive beneficial spillovers from some transnational public goods, and, in so doing, can increase the number of potential contributors. A country that does not have the capacity to benefit from a public good cannot be expected to support its provision.

The remainder of the chapter consists of six primary sections. The first section is devoted to presenting a more carefully drawn definition of public goods and in distinguishing among various kinds of public goods. The ensuing section presents two classification schemes for public goods: the first is based on the spatial range of spillovers (i.e., which countries benefit) and the type of the public good; and the second is dependent on the spillover range and the manner in which individual contributions determine the overall level of the public good. In the third section, the relationship between development assistance and international public goods is explored, along with the relationship between international public good development assistance and more traditional forms of aid. Institutional considerations are examined in the fourth section. The fifth section expands the institutional discussion by investigating the subsidiarity rationale for choosing which institution is most appropriate for supplying international public goods. The final section indicates some policy recommendations and concluding remarks.

. . . .

PUBLIC GOODS: DEFINITIONS AND TYPES

■   PUBLIC GOODS, AND INTERNATIONAL PUBLIC GOODS in particular, differ in terms of the reach of their benefits, the characteristics of these benefits, and how the overall level of the goods depends on individual contributions. Each of these aspects must be understood if the proper policy decisions are to be taken when giving development assistance in the form of international public goods. The nature of the international public good also determines who should and will provide the good. We must resist the temptation to lump these goods into a single class that abides by one set of policy recommendations. Thus, an in-depth focus on these goods' characteristics is necessary.

PURE AND IMPURE PUBLIC GOODS

The term *public good* is misleading because "public" does not necessarily imply that a government must supply the good. Some public goods (e.g., national defense) are indeed provided by the government, whereas others (e.g., satellite communications, extension services) may be offered by the private sector or by both the private and public sectors. Public here means that the goods' benefits possess two properties that distinguish these goods from those that can be traded in markets: they are *nonexcludable*, meaning there is no affordable way to extract payment from the beneficiaries; and there is *nonrivalry of benefits*, meaning one user's consumption does not diminish the benefits available to others. Consider these properties in terms of a *pure public good*. The benefits of a pure public good are available to everyone—payers and nonpayers alike—once the good is provided; that is, its benefits are *nonexcludable*. This inability to exclude limits incentives on the part of users to finance the good's provision, thus leading users to take a "free ride" on the provision efforts of others. If, for example, the United Nations restores peace in a developing country plagued by an ethnic conflict, then neighboring countries at risk from the conflict spreading cannot be excluded from the increased stability and reduced threat derived from this peacekeeping. Similarly, eradicating a pest in a developing country yields benefits to all in danger, regardless of who supports this action.

Nations are anticipated to undercontribute to international pure public goods unless they form collectives (e.g., alliances, international networks, treaties) to coordinate their contributions. The proper-sized collective would include all, and only, those nations receiving benefits from a specific international public good. When the public good's benefit range exceeds the geographical region of the provision-deciding collective, too little is produced because benefits conferred on nonmember countries are not included in the collective's provision decision. If, in contrast, the good's benefit range is smaller than the collective's combined area, too much of the good is then anticipated as taxes are collected from those who do not benefit from the good.[9] That is, the collective abuses its taxing authority and burdens nations outside the range of spillovers with financing the public good. Unless the decision-making body's jurisdiction precisely matches the countries affected by the public good's benefits and costs, there is no assurance that the good's provision will properly equate the requisite benefits to the associated costs.

The second distinguishing property of a pure public good is *nonrivalry of benefits*. Nonrivalry results when one user's consumption of the good does not detract, in the slightest, from the consumption opportunities still available to others from the *same* unit of the good. Limiting the accumulation of greenhouse gases in the atmosphere provides nonrival benefits worldwide. Similarly, the cleansing of a river can be enjoyed by all developing nations along its banks; one nation's enjoyment of the cleaner environment does not decrease the benefits available to others. The cure for a disease also yields nonrival benefits insofar as applying the cure to one person does not inhibit its application to others. By the same token, the development and deployment of more productive agricultural procedures provide nonrival benefits. When benefits are nonrival, it is inefficient to exclude anyone who derives a positive benefit,[10] because extending consumption to more users creates benefits that cost society nothing.

It must be noted, however, that a public good may not confer positive benefits on all recipients. For instance, fluoridated water is viewed by some as harmful. These individuals must incur a cost in terms of buying bottled water to avoid drinking the treated water. Fluoridation is, nonetheless, a public good if most potential recipients consider it beneficial. Eliminating an organized crime threat is a public good even though the criminals and those who profit from their activities are hurt by this elimination.

Pure public goods display both nonrival and nonexcludable benefits. Other examples include finding a cure to malaria, alleviating air pollutants, limiting ozone shield thinning, and applying sound financial practices. When a public good possesses benefits that are either partially nonrival or partially excludable (i.e., excludable at a cost), then the good is *impurely public*. If one user's consumption of the public good detracts from the quality or quantity of benefits available to others, then benefits are partially nonrival. Crowding (or congestion) is a likely form of this detraction or rivalry, and can result in longer queues for medical attention, slower transits along a highway, reductions in extension assistance, or thinning of military forces along a front. An important subclass of impure public goods consists of *club goods*, (e.g., transportation networks, sporting events), which possess partially rival benefits that can be excluded at an affordable cost.

ON CLUBS

If exclusion costs are sufficiently small to allow utilization rates to be monitored and users to be charged a *toll* or user fee, then the users can form a collective, called a *club*, and provide themselves with the shared good.[11] Club goods—communication networks, irrigation systems, extension services, common markets, military alliances, the electromagnetic spectrum, nature preserves—can be provided by members and financed through tolls imposed on members that charge for the crowding costs at the margin. Unlike pure public goods, club goods can be allocated efficiently by the club members since the toll mechanism can force payments that *"internalize"* or account for the crowding externality. In so doing, resources for providing club goods are directed to their most valued use. Even taste differences among members are taken into account: members with a stronger preference for the club good will visit more often and will thus pay more in total tolls. A club represents a clever institutional arrangement for getting users, through their use, to indicate how much value they place on the good and to be charged accordingly. For example, users of a satellite communication network who gain the most from signals sent will utilize the network most often and pay the greatest charges. In contrast, nonexcludable public goods (e.g., better air quality) do not provide a means for monitoring and charging for the good's use.

Clubs can form at different political levels: At the national level, clubs can allocate resources to recreation facilities, school districts, transportation systems, and parks. Subnational jurisdictions (e.g., townships and provinces) are clubs that provide a whole package of club goods. Similarly, nations can join a club to share an excludable public good without sacrificing sovereignty over taxing or other fiscal functions to a supranational government structure. In a club, member states must only agree to pay tolls for the shared good on an as-needed basis. INTELSAT, a private consortium of nations and firms as members, operates as a club to share a communication satellite network that carries most international phone calls and television signals.[12] Even the deployment of crisis-management squads to a terrorist incident or a regional instability can be operated as a club. Perhaps the best instance of the latter was Desert Storm in 1991 for which Kuwait, Saudi Arabia, and the United Arab Emirates financed much of the U.S.-led mission with the rest paid by Germany and Japan, which are heavily dependent on Middle East oil.[13]

When exclusion is practical, clubs represent a desirable institutional alternative to forming or relying on governmental bodies, which must finance the shared good through taxes. Often these taxes sever the connection between who receives the goods' benefits and who finances them, thus resulting in allocative inefficiency. Clubs economize on transaction costs while they minimize members' losses of autonomy. We shall return to the use of clubs with respect to some forms of development assistance when addressing institutional considerations.

JOINT PRODUCTS

Another relevant class of public goods for the study of development assistance includes those activities that yield two or more outputs or *joint products*, which may vary in their degree of publicness. As such, joint product outputs may be purely public, private, or impurely public. For example, a military alliance can through its formidable forces yield deterrence, an *alliance-wide* pure public good. If an enemy is kept from attacking, all allies gain from this deterrence. Because an alliance's arsenal and forces can also be used to provide disaster relief, coastal protection, and anti-insurgency actions, *ally-specific* benefits are also jointly derived from the same military assets. Tied development assistance also represents a joint product activity. By alleviating a recipient's poverty or improving its health through the provision of infrastructure (e.g., a sewer system in Cairo), tied development assistance yields public benefits in the form of altruism to the world. If, in return, the donor also obtains one or more country-specific benefits (e.g., military bases or political support in world forums), then this donor's charity will be motiviated beyond altruistic gains. The greater is the share of country-specific private benefits to all benefits received from the activity, the more allocatively efficient will be the provision of the activity.[14] When all benefits are country-specific (private) goods, markets can operate so that donor and recipient countries can engage in exchanges.

Joint products also characterize the rain forests, whose preservation generates purely public benefits worldwide owing to carbon sequestration and biodiversity. Host-country and regional benefits from these forests include erosion control, localized climate effects, watersheds, and ecotourist sites. These localized benefits give these tropical countries a stake or ownership in their forest preservation and, in so doing, should motivate some preservation. When determining development assistance to preserve these forests, donors must remember that these host-country benefits also motivate preservation on the host country's own behalf. Merck's agreement to pay the National Biodiversity Institute of Costa Rica a million dollars for "prospecting" rights for useful plant chemicals and extracts from the country's rain forest represents a means for augmenting these host-country benefits.[15]

Aid-assisted family planning also yields joint products. By limiting population size, there is less growth in energy demands which, in turns, implies worldwide public good benefits from a slower increase in greenhouse gas emissions and global warming.[16] In addition, country-specific benefits follow from the enhanced quality of life that family planning can entail. These benefits may include endogenous growth effects as women have access to greater educational opportunities when childbearing is put off until a later age.

In the case of charitable giving within countries, charities frequently create donor-specific benefits to increase contribution and circumvent free riding.[17] Thus, season tickets are given to supporters of a ballet company; buildings are named after large contributors to universities; charity shipments display the donor country's name; and plaques are erected listing major donors to museums. If the donor-specific benefits are complementary to the public benefit conferred, then contributions from others are not apt to eliminate donors' desire to make their own donations. Complementary goods are best consumed together in which each good enhances the benefits derived from the other good (e.g., bread and butter). In essence, these donor-specific benefits establish some property rights (i.e., ownership claim) to the contributions in the name of the donor and, in so doing, allow donors to view their efforts *not as substitutes* for the efforts of others. Complementarity of these donor-specific and general public benefits may actually motivate a donor to give more as others give more, because greater public benefit spillovers require that there be more donor-specific benefits, which can only be had by one's own donations.[18] Development assistance does not have to be conditional to display these donor-specific joint products. If a donor derives status in the world community from its development assistance activities, then donor-specific benefits are present without aid being tied. Substantial efforts by the Scandinavian countries and their aid-giving institutions may be partly motivated by the status provided by these relatively large development assistance efforts. The European Union's (EU) contributions to the transition economies of Eastern Europe may also result in greater trading opportunities for the contributors. Joint products have important implications for policy decisions regarding the type of development assistance that works best when trying to provide international public goods. If, for example, a large share of benefits derived from a public good (e.g., a rain forest) is donor-specific and/or recipient-specific, then the parties should be able to consummate an efficient agreement on their own.

Joint products also have important implications for the *neutrality result* that hampers attempts to use income redistribution or tax-financed support of public goods to increase the provision of the pure public good.[19] Quite simply, the neutrality result states that a redistribution of income among contributors (whose tastes can differ) has no net effect on public good supply; those receiving income increase their public good contributions by precisely the amount that those losing income decrease their contributions. Suppose that two nations are cutting greenhouse gas emissions. Further suppose that nation A has a greater propensity to reduce these emissions than nation B. A supranational authority interested in engineering greater emission cuts may attempt to do so by redistributing income from nation B to nation A. Unfortunately, this will not have any effect on emissions, because nation B will decrease its emission-reducing efforts owing to the income loss by precisely the amount that income-recipient nation A increases its efforts. Moreover, any attempt by a government (or multilateral institution) to increase the supply of a pure public good by taxing contributors and using these funds to supply the public good also fails as contributors reduce their expenditures on the good by exactly the amount of their new taxes.

These outcomes hinge on the pure publicness of the good and the manner in which each unit contributed adds equally to the total supply.[20] Because one contributor's provision of the pure public good is a *perfect substitute* for that from another contributor, increased provision, however financed, replaces the need to contribute these units on one's own. With pure public goods, contributors view public good benefit spillovers from others equivalently to extra income, so that nations can maintain their well-being by letting increased public good efforts by others make up for their income losses. Because pure public goods are in short supply, one naturally wants to turn to an income redistribution or taxing policy (known as an *income policy*) to rectify the shortfall. But neutrality indicates that this intuition is wrong for the standard pure public good. A government would have to tax noncontributors in order to augment public good supply, because the noncontributors cannot reduce their public good contributions in reaction to the tax. Unfortunately, this taxation policy may not be welfare improving if these noncontributor's welfare is adversely affected by the tax-and-spend policy.[21] An adverse effect is anticipated when noncontributors have little taste for the public good that they are now forced to support.

These policy difficulties also apply to development assistance in the form of purely public goods even when the donor goes first and the recipient follows with its supplemental support.[22] If, however, joint products apply, then neutrality no longer plagues income policies because contributions are no longer perfectly substitutable, making it possible to engineer redistributions that have a net positive effect on foreign-aid-assisted activities that are jointly produced. For example, assessment-financed development assistance through multilateral agencies need not result in offsetting declines in direct donor assistance when there are jointly produced *donor-specific* benefits. In the case of recipient countries, recipient-specific benefits serve an "ownership" function that motivates the recipient's own efforts even in the presence of outside assistance. These efforts can, for example, result in the recipient coming up with recurrent costs associated with many aid projects. An absence of this ownership property is recognized as a key weakness in past development assistance to Africa.[23] Thus, joint products represent a promising class of public goods in the case of development assistance. In some instances, the jointly produced benefits may be a club good, thus allowing a club arrangement to address its allocation if the club benefit is a relatively large share of total benefits.

. . . .

PUBLIC GOODS CLASSIFICATION SCHEMES

■   PUBLIC GOODS REPRESENT A RICH SET OF ACTIVITIES that vary according to a number of dimensions. There are, thus, myriad ways of classifying public goods. Any such taxonomy requires judgments as to the important properties of these goods to highlight.

TYPES OF PUBLIC GOODS

The first scheme presented associates a spatial range of benefit spillovers to the four kinds of public goods just identified. The spatial dimension is included owing to our interest to develop a subsidiarity theory of assistance, based on spatial and jurisdictional considerations. The four classes of goods relate to the properties of the good's benefits (i.e., nonrivalry and nonexcludability). In Table 1, there are 12 categories of public goods identified along with two examples of each. Examples are chosen that have relevance for development assistance recipients. The columns indicate the four classes of public goods, while the rows represent the goods' range of spillovers—national, regional (e.g., East Africa), or global. At the national level, groundwater purification and defense represent pure public goods. Another example of a national pure public good is agricultural research findings that are specific to a country's geoclimatic conditions. Goods generating nonrival and nonexcludable benefits for a well-identified region are regional pure public goods. Eliminating pests indigenous to a region or curing a tropical disease are examples, since the gains are to multiple countries but not to the world at large. Benefit spillovers are, however, global for reducing global warming or stratospheric ozone depletion by cutting down on greenhouse gases and CFCs, respectively. Given global investment markets, the institution of sound financial practices in almost any country can benefit investors everywhere by curbing potential financial instabilities and their contagion. Sounder accounting, financial, and banking practices in Indonesia or Japan benefit investors worldwide. Obviously, finer geographical or jurisdictional distinctions for the national and regional categories could be made.

Waterways and transportation networks are impurely public at the national level, because congestion grows as utilization increases. Immunization is impurely public at the regional level because its benefits decline as propinquity decreases; people nearer to one another are more apt to experience the reduced risks offered by immunization. Likewise, acid rain is impure because its dispersion is based on a spatial rivalry—the further countries are from the source of the sulfur or nitrogen oxide emissions, the less of these emissions remain in the atmosphere to be deposited on them.[24]

At the global level, similar spatial aspects affect curbing organized crime or the ability to contain a disease.

Six club goods are also listed in the table. Club goods are a subclass of impure public goods whose partially rival benefits are excludable by the provider. For example, agricultural extension services can be withheld from nonpayers. As one client obtains these services, there are less available to others unless these services are disseminated by television or a similar medium. These services can be provided in a club arrangement on a user-fee basis. Congestion in an irrigation system involves both the volume of water flow and siltation. Crowding in terms of signal interference characterizes communication networks and INTELSAT, in particular. Common markets can lead to rivalry as either funds must be spread over more projects, or more sellers vie for the same pool of customers. Tourists can be charged tolls when visiting rain forests and other natural wonders, based on the crowding they cause.

Finally, six examples of joint products with alternative extents of benefit spillovers are indicated in Table 1. Joint products have outputs that include one or more of the three basic kinds of public goods in the first three columns. Jointness is a matter of degree. If a public good or the elimination of a public bad primarily provides a purely public benefit (e.g., reducing global warming), then we place it in the pure public category. When, however, multiple outputs are prevalent, the activity is characterized as having joint products. For example, the development of civil services provides private benefits to service recipients as well as countrywide benefits when this development coordinates activities among provinces. By lessening threats to neighboring countries, peacekeeping activities yield regionwide public benefits along with country-specific benefits to the crisis-laden nation. Cleansing a lake can benefit not only the countries along its banks but also other nearby countries that gain from the lake's recreational and tourist attractions. Improved labor standards not only raise the welfare of workers in developing countries instituting them, but they also improve welfare worldwide as higher standards in developing countries relieve downward pressures on these standards in developed countries.[25]

In summary, Table 1 serves two purposes for this policy essay. First, it emphasizes that the reach of the good's benefit spillovers may vary and, in so doing, the relevant participants or institution involved in providing the public good should match these spillover ranges.[26] Second, the type of public good indicates that the appropriate policy and institutional arrangement

TABLE 1. PUBLIC GOODS CLASSIFIED
BY TYPE

Spillover Range	Pure Public	Impure Public	Club	Joint Products
National	• groundwater purification • defense	• waterways • transporation grids	• communication networks • irrigation systems	• civil services • education
Regional	• malaria cure • pest eradication	• immunization programs • acid rain reduction	• common markets • extension services	• peacekeeping • cleansing a lake
Global	• global warming • financial practices	• curbing organized crime • controlling disease	• ecotourist sites • INTELSAT	• labor standards • forest protection

differ. The incentive to contribute and, hence, the need to institute policy hinge on these classes of goods.

ANOTHER DIMENSION OF PUBLICNESS: AGGREGATION TECHNOLOGIES

A second classification scheme addresses the fact that the manner in which individual contributions to the public good determine the total quantity of the good available for consumption varies among different goods. In some cases, this total equals the sum of everyone's contributions, while, in other cases, the total may equal either the smallest or the largest contribution. The relationship between individual contributions and the overall level of the public good is henceforth called the *aggregation technology* and represents another feature that influences aid policy effectiveness with respect to public goods.[27]

SUMMATION. The most common such technology is *summation* where each unit contributed to the public good adds equally to the overall level of the good. A unit contributed by anyone has the same additional impact on the total provision, so that the contribution of one agent serves as a perfect substitute for that of another. The summation technology with its substitutability implication is largely responsible for the difficulties, discussed earlier, that hamper the ability of income policies to correct for the underprovision of a public good. An example of this technology is given in Table 2 for each of the three ranges of spillovers.[28] Tropospheric or surface-level ozone pollution in cities from vehicles and other sources abides by the summation technology, so that efforts to reduce these emissions affect tropospheric concentrations of pollutants in an additive fashion. The accumulation of greenhouse gases also adheres to an additive technology of aggregation. If each of five nations emits 1000 metric tons of these gases into the atmosphere, global warming will be affected by 5000 additional metric tons in the atmosphere. At the regional level, stemming the spread of deserts (i.e., desertification) through better land-use practices is determined by the sum of neighboring nations' efforts.[29]

Consider the policy implications of curbing global warming. Given the summation technology, one country's efforts to stem greenhouse gas emissions merely substitute for those of another. This means that direct income transfers by developed countries to developing countries in the hopes that greenhouse gas emissions will fall worldwide is not necessarily an effective policy. If, however, the recipient country can reduce emissions *cheaper* than the donor country, then the transfer is effective in curbing worldwide emissions. Once efficiency differences exist, the substitution of provision activities between transferrer and transferee is no longer on a one-for-one basis. In this case, direct support of curbing emissions would be better than a general income transfer. Given the carbon-dirty technologies in many developing countries, it may be cheaper initially to get a greater return on money targeted to reducing such emissions there.

BEST SHOT. A second aggregation technology is *"best-shot"* for which the level of the public good equals the largest (individual) provision level. In confronting a within-country terrorist threat, the particular police force that exerts the largest effort can do the most to neutralize the group. The greatest contribution or effort also determines the overall level of the public good when developing a pest-resistant crop or disarming a rogue nation. To find a cure for malaria, AIDS, or other diseases, the research team exerting

TABLE 2. PUBLIC GOODS CLASSIFIED BY THE AGGREGATION TECHNOLOGY

Spillover Range	Summation	Best Shot	Weakest Link	Weighted Sum
National	• curbing urban air pollution	• neutralizing terrorists	• protecting against insurrections	• limiting run-off pollution
Regional	• alleviating desertification	• curing malaria	• toxic waste containment	• acid rain reduction
Global	• global warming	• curing AIDS	• disease containment	• nuclear accident fallout

the largest effort is typically the one that meets with success. Once a cure is found, it can potentially benefit everyone, even those whose efforts fell short of finding the cure. In a development assistance context, best-shot activities often imply that the developed countries should not transfer resources to developing countries, but, instead, provide the activities at home and then allow the associated spillover benefits to be received by others. For instance, research efforts must be concentrated where the breakthrough is most likely, which is apt to be in developed countries. Research moneys and efforts geared to best-shot discoveries should not be dispersed as a form of development assistance.[30] By doing the research themselves, the developed countries also avoid an "agency" problem when the recipient does not use the assistance for its intended purpose.

WEAKEST LINK. *"Weakest-link"* represents a third basic aggregation technology where the smallest contribution fixes the effective public good level of the group. When a nation is confronted with an insurrection, the province with the least effective defense will set the safety standard for the entire nation. Similarly, the country with the smallest offensive against containing a disease through immunization or prophylactic actions determines the chances, for all at risk, of quarantining and eliminating the disease. Ineffective efforts to eradicate tuberculosis in poor countries meant that the disease could return in a more virulent form to rich countries during the 1990s. Containing toxic wastes at the regional level also abides by a weakest-link technology. For weakest-link, matching behavior characterizes the anticipated equilibrium, insofar as contributions beyond the smallest do nothing to augment the level of the public good and result in less consumption. For *normal* public goods (i.e., those whose consumption increases with income), the smallest contribution is that of the poorest nation. In contrast, only the richest nation contributes to best-shot public goods.[31] Even for the summation technology, there is a marked tendency for the contributors to be the richer countries,[32] because as these nations provide the good, the poorer countries desired amount of the public good are attained so that they can free ride. As the number of countries increase, this tendency is reinforced. With a sufficient number of countries and enough income disparity, only the richest country will support some public goods that abide by the summation technology.[33]

Weakest-link public goods, such as disease containment, have a couple of important implications for development assistance in the form of international public goods. Because the smallest level of the public good determines the level experienced by all countries receiving spillovers, donor countries must bring up the level of disease containment in all countries whose levels are judged inadequate. This is an expensive proposition. Moreover, direct provision of the good is more effective than an income transfer, since the latter is expected to be used for some other purposes by the recipient than just providing the disease containment. There is therefore an apparent tension between the two approaches of this policy essay. When weakest-link public goods (e.g., containing the spread of Ebola) represent a clear and present danger, and the country does not possess the capacity to implement the common pool approach, arrangements to directly provide the weakest-link good outside the common pool may be justified. If there is no such exigency, then the weakest-link public good should be funded through the common pool procedure.

WEIGHTED SUM. A fourth aggregate technology is *weighted sum* for which weights are applied to the individual contributions before summing them. This technology is a generalization of the summation technology, which corresponds to the case where all weights are one. Acid rain deposition and its reduction adhere to this technology at the regional level (see Table 2). The deposition on country i is the weighted sum of the emissions of the other countries, where these weights are the share of other countries' emissions deposited on country i. Corresponding weights depend on wind direction, the countries' relative location, their sizes, and other considerations. At the global level, fallout from nuclear accidents (e.g., Chernobyl) is an example of a weighted-sum technology. Nations downwind and nearer to the accident received the lion share of the fallout. Eventually, the released radioactive substances were dispersed worldwide with large differences in concentrations among recipients. This heterogeneous dispersion results in diverse incentives to take action. Richer nations and those whose weights are the largest are the likely contributors. Limiting pollution run-off from fields similarly corresponds to this technology but at a much more localized level.

When the weights are not one, the weighted-sum technology will not necessarily be associated with a difficulty to correct for the underprovision of the public good through income transfers and public provision. This follows because public good contributions in one country are no longer perfect substitutes for those in another country. The country's own share of its contribution motivates it to act, because this share indicates the country's "ownership" to the consequences of its public good contribution. When its share is one and others' shares are zero, the activity is really a private good and optimal action should ensue. As the country's own share increases, it acquires a greater stake in its contributions, since the resulting benefit is "privatized"; that is, the country cannot receive these benefits unless it contributes. Redistribution of income from those with smaller shares to those with larger shares serves to increase the level of the public good.

In a development context, peacekeeping efforts may confer benefits in a weighted-sum manner based on spatial propinquity, with contiguous countries benefiting the most. When this is the case, countries in the immediate region have the most to gain from peacekeeping and are expected to provide the forces. As a country develops, benefits are conferred on its trading partners, so that potential trade-derived benefits from development assistance involve trading shares. Nations with greater such trading shares are more motivated to underwrite this development assistance.

Although there are more than four basic aggregation technologies, these four are sufficient for the purposes of this policy essay, because they are the most relevant ones for the international public goods associated with development. The introduction of technologies other than summation serves a number of policy insights. First, by not implying perfect substitutability among contributions, these alternative technologies indicate that there is a role for development assistance in addressing under-provision. Moreover, assistance from nongovernmental organizations need not crowd out government-based assistance or the recipient's own efforts. Second, these technologies yield diverse implications for the anticipated source of development assistance as the disparity between the poorest and the richest countries increases (see the next section). Third, alternative aggregation technologies influence whether the developed country should supply the public good to these developing countries, or provide it at home and allow the benefits to spill over. Fourth, the principle of subsidiarity developed in a later section is influenced by these underlying aggregation technologies. Fifth, these aggregation technologies influence the incentives of donor countries to support the international public goods in developing countries. For some weakest-link public goods, donor countries may have no choice but to supply the public good if they want to keep their own people's welfare levels high. For weighted sum, donors' weighted benefits may be sufficiently large to ensure the public good's provision.

· ·

THE RELATIONSHIP BETWEEN DEVELOPMENT AND INTERNATIONAL PUBLIC GOODS

■   THE INTERFACE BETWEEN DEVELOPMENT and international public goods is complex—these public goods help support development, while a country's stage of development influences cross-border spillovers.

ARE INTERNATIONAL PUBLIC GOODS NEEDED FOR DEVELOPMENT?

Even Adam Smith, a champion of laissez-faire, recognized the need for government provision in four areas: the establishment of a justice system; the enactment and enforcement of laws; the protection against invasion; and the provision of schools, transportation networks, and other public goods. If markets are to function, an infrastructure is needed to allow for the voluntary exchange of property rights. This infrastructure also raises up a country's capacity to gain from some public goods (e.g., scientific breakthroughs). The establishment of the requisite infrastructure, including the means for defining and enforcing property rights, represents a public good whose benefits are nonrival and nonexcludable (i.e., pure public good). The transition economies of Eastern Europe and the emerging-market economies of Asia, Africa, and South America must provide this infrastructure if these economies are to become full-fledged market economies. Part of this infrastructure includes sound financial and accounting practices so that investors can properly judge alternative investment opportunities. Interest rates must, like any opportunity cost, reflect scarcity value so that financial capital can flow to its best opportunity. Sound macroeconomic and monetary policies along with a well-managed central banking system constitute other integral pieces of this infrastructure. Proper financial practices and sensible policies in these emerging-market economies also influence development and economic growth in developed countries, whose companies sell to these markets. Hence, these practices and policies provide nonrival and nonexcludable benefits worldwide, and are, thus, international pure public goods. Recent financial crises in Japan, Indonesia, Malaysia, South Korea, and elsewhere highlight the negative cross-border effects that can radiate worldwide from shortcomings in this financial and macroeconomic infrastructure. The interest in globalization and investing in emerging-market economies means that failures in these economies can destabilize investment markets half a world away. Consequently, it is in everyone's interest that developing economies establish a sound financial infrastructure, compatible and comparable to those of the developed countries.

Other international public goods (e.g., reduced urban pollution, improved disease control, better sanitation) in developing countries not only increase these countries' welfare but can also promote their development and growth. For example, city environments free of lead pollutants make for smarter children. Similarly, urban centers with lower pollution levels will have more productive labor forces. Many international public goods are essential for productive and healthy people in developing countries and abroad.

In some developing countries, solutions to a host of public bads are essential to attract foreign direct investment (FDI), which provides much-needed savings to underwrite development. FDI also serves as a channel for the transfer of technological spillovers, embodied in the equipment brought to the host country.[34] International public bads that inhibit FDI include terrorism, inadequate contract laws, poor food safety, diseases, and others. Consider the possible impact of a terrorist campaign on FDI. When deciding whether to invest in a foreign country, a potential investor is concerned about the expected return and risk associated with a contemplated investment relative to other opportunities at home and abroad. If terrorist attacks are directed at foreign investment and personnel, then perceived risks and costs increase. Even if the attacks are not directed at FDI, the collateral damage may be significant. These risks and adverse consequences may be heightened if terrorists attack the military, the country's officials, the airports, the courts, or other symbols of the establishment.[35] Such attacks weaken the market-promoting infrastructure. If terrorist threats are ameliorated, then an international public good and its benefit spillovers are directly provided to the host country as well as to investing countries. Improved food and water safety can also attract FDI by creating a healthier environment for the personnel required by the FDI. Peacekeeping operations targeted at ending a civil war can also foster the necessary environment for FDI. As such, this promotion of FDI is a joint product of these peacekeeping efforts.

If a conducive environment for FDI is supplied by development assistance or the country's own efforts, then the inflow of private investment from home and abroad lessens the future need for development assistance. Without the requisite public goods and infrastructure to support a market economy, development will be inhibited. Components of this infrastructure that are club goods (e.g., communication networks, financial intermediaries, agricultural extension services) can be provided by private firms or collectives. A crucial insight is the realization that not all infrastructure must come from governments. Those components where exclusion is impossible or inadvisable (e.g., a justice system, defense, property right enforcement) have to be provided publicly. However, by relying on the private sector for some infrastructure and public goods, the public sector will be able to channel its scarce resources into those public goods where private incentives do not exist.

The presence of transnational spillovers from public goods required to promote market transactions means that developed countries have an interest to help provide these goods. This self-interest is strengthened when resulting spillovers possess some donor-specific benefits. Despite this self-interest, donors of all types must successfully address strong incentives to free ride on the development assistance contributed by others. This underscores a need for development assistance providers to coordinate their responses so that free riding and project duplication are avoided. In this regard, there is a complementarity between the two approaches of this essay, since the common pool can be used to fund some public goods while coordinating donors' efforts. Engineering donor-specific joint products or selective incentives is one way of motivating donors.[36]

IS DEVELOPMENT NEEDED FOR INTERNATIONAL PUBLIC GOODS?

Just as international public goods are needed for development, development is also required to support the provision of these public goods and ameliorate international public bads. Without development, poverty will lead to health problems, civil unrest, famine, and environmental degradation (e.g., acid rain). These public bads can create cross-border spillovers that harm neighboring countries and beyond. Development can provide a domestic tax base from which to finance international public goods and eliminate international public bads. Growth and development can also create their own public bads (e.g., pollution). By raising the standard of living, development directly mitigates some of these public bads. For example, the demand for better air quality and a less polluted environment responds positively to income; richer countries spend more on maintaining a clean environment.[37] As a country develops, it is also better equipped to take advantage of the benefits of public good spillovers from abroad. Although pure public goods' benefits are nonexcludable, not all recipients possess the requisite background or capacity to gain from these spillovers. Training, education, and technology are thus required for developing countries to take advantage of many international public good spillovers. Some public goods are a prerequisite before others can be beneficial. This implies sequential considerations when introducing public goods into developing countries; if the proper foundation is not instituted, some public goods will have little effect. The effective range or reach of spillovers may then hinge on a proper foundation being laid in recipient countries, so that their capacity to benefit from public goods is achieved. Traditional development assistance can foster this capacity building.

INTERNATIONAL PUBLIC GOODS AS DEVELOPMENT ASSISTANCE

The development discourse has been enriched, and complicated considerably, by increased recognition of issues to do with cross-border spillovers and international public goods. It can be argued that this recognition is nothing other than a return to an earlier period, where the founders of the postwar international order were keenly aware from the experience of the 1930s of the problems that interdependence between nation-states could create for all states if not managed. This earlier interest was directed at just a few public goods: the international financial system, world poverty, and world health. Today's focus on international public goods is more pervasive and involves almost every facet of economic and human activity—e.g., labor standards, the environment, research, financial practices, health, security, and contract law.

In the past, development assistance primarily addressed country-specific development issues; however, novel international public goods and their wide dispersion of spillover benefits suggest that development assistance may increasingly assume the form of public goods. There are many instances of development assistance in this form, such as the activities of the U.S. Centers for Disease Control to monitor and contain new diseases. Efforts to restore peace in developing countries also denote aid-related public goods, for which budgets have grown from $200-300 million per year in the 1970s and 1980s to $3-6 billion in the 1990s.[38] Technical assistance, pledged by the developed countries in the Montreal Protocol on ozone-depleting substances, to assist these countries in substituting CFCs with more benign substances also represents a multilaterally provided international public good.[39] Other examples include immunizing populations, disseminating technological breakthroughs, monitoring the atmosphere, and containing radioactive wastes. Actions by developed countries to introduce laws governing exchange in the transition economies are other aid-financed public goods. Support given to countries (e.g., Angola, Cambodia, Haiti) to build up their institutions and infrastructure during a transition period to democracy yields international public goods in terms of peace, security, and improved welfare, underwritten by development assistance.

Technology is anticipated to continue to produce novel forms of public goods and bads that draw nations of the world closer together in terms of the economic consequences of their activities. Much of these new technologies will be developed by a handful of rich countries. Consider public goods derived from space-based activities, including satellites and the next space lab. The ability of the new generation of weather satellites to see inside of hurricanes generates more accurate predictions of storm severity, so that better preparations to safeguard populations can avert the huge human toll like that of Hurricane Mitch in Honduras and Nicaragua during 1998. Findings regarding the aging process from space-lab research can be used to improve everyone's well-being. Advancements in computer technology, remote sensing, biotechnology, toxic waste removal, environmental cleanup, and security systems are expected to be developed in the richest nations, from which they can be supplied to developing countries.

Current trends in income inequality are anticipated to increase the *proportion* of development assistance that takes the form of international public goods. Between 1960 and 1994, the richest fifth of all nations had their share of world income rise from 70.0 percent to 85.8 percent, while the poorest fifth had their shares fall from 2.3 percent to 1.1 percent.[40] This gap between the two poles of the income distribution spectrum continues to widen despite some improved shares within the spectrum by some of the emerging-market economies. There are many underlying factors behind this widening gulf between the richest and poorest countries. These include innovations being concentrated in the richest countries; the transfer of ill-suited technologies to the poorer countries; political instabilities and civil wars plaguing the poorest countries; autocratic regimes siphoning off resources for their extravagant lifestyle; and limited savings to support investment.[41]

There is every indication that countries, particularly the rich, are becoming "fatigued" with traditional development assistance, preferring instead private capital flows to finance development.[42] This fatigue may be bolstered by the realization that some development assistance merely enriches corrupt regimes and bureaucrats, and does not necessarily benefit the poor for whom it is intended. Another source of this fatigue, now and into the future, stems from an ever-increasing provision of international public goods by the richest echelon of nations. This is already evident in these nations' efforts to address environmental, health, security, and monitoring concerns. Solutions to future exigencies involving best-shot public goods, whose level is primarily based on the largest contribution, will generally be provided by the richest countries. Thus, a select group of nations will develop cures to diseases, disarm rogue nations, limit the proliferation of weapons of mass destruction, retrieve deadly pollutants, provide research breakthroughs, restore environmental quality, and monitor the planet. Their provision will confer *"free-rider aid"* on other countries. Even for a summation aggregation technology, the richest countries are expected to be the greatest contributors to these public goods and, in some cases, the only contributor.

This pattern of increasing free-rider aid is also expected to characterize weakest-link public goods. The growing income disparity between the richest and poorest nations implies that the weakest-link nation's provision level will fall relative to the desired level of these public goods in the richest country. To bring the smallest contribution level up to an adequate level, the richest country will either have to subsidize the weakest-link contributors or else directly provide the public good for them. This can be an expensive proposition when a large number of nations can only afford a small amount of a public good whose minimum contribution fixes the level of the good for everyone. Thus, efforts to contain diseases, pests, or deadly contaminants may have to be provided or financed by just a rich group of nations. When trying to contain a disease, rich countries might *initially* have to dispatch medical teams to a weakest-link developing country. But over time, public good development assistance to contain diseases in such a country must build up the country's own medical capacity to treat and contain diseases if this country's weakest-link status is ever to change. Recent actions by the United States to keep weapon-grade plutonium in the Ukraine and other former Soviet republics from falling into the wrong hands illustrate a case of direct provision of a weakest-link public good. The United States went in to dismantle and dispose of warheads so that sufficient safeguards were applied. The efforts of the United States and EU countries to capture shipments of plutonium from Eastern Europe are yet another action to address a weakest-link public good problem by providing containment for the world.

This anticipated increase in development assistance in the form of public goods should be politically acceptable to the electorate in donor nations for a number of reasons. First, the provision of these international public goods will directly benefit the donor's electorate. A healthier African and Asian population will, for example, mean less transmission of diseases to the developed world. Second, when development assistance is given in the form of an international public good, it cannot pad the pockets of corrupt leaders or officials. The "aid" is spent by the donor in providing the public good, and there is no agency problem. Third, there may exist donor-specific jointly produced benefits that can also motivate action (e.g., employment opportunities associated with supplying the public good). Fourth, when given as an international public good, the development assistance is disguised making it more acceptable to the donor's electorate. Fifth, for weakest-link and best-shot scenarios, the donor country may not really have a choice if the consequences of not giving the required level of the good are sufficiently dire.

Development assistance in the form of international public goods will have to be supplemented with other forms of conventional development assistance in a common-pool arrangement (see Chapter 3). Although public good development assistance addresses some underlying factors of poverty, it does not provide basic needs to feed, clothe, and educate the poor when the resulting benefit spillovers are modest. These more traditional development assistance activities are necessary if developing countries are to acquire the capacity to provide international public goods and profit from the benefit spillovers of such goods, when provided abroad. Public good development assistance also does not finance infrastructure in the expanding urban centers. Essentially, international public good development assistance will be directed at those problems where cross-border spillovers are the greatest.

. . . .

INSTITUTIONAL CONSIDERATIONS

■ DEVELOPMENT ASSISTANCE CAN COME DIRECTLY from donor countries, indirectly from donor country support of multilateral agencies, or directly from private donor agencies. Which of these sources should supply the development assistance in the form of public goods? Given the pressures that the electorate in donor countries will place on their governments to alleviate negative cross-border spillovers from developing countries, some of these cross-border concerns will be handled directly by donor governments. Also, the scale of operations required to cope with some of these public good problems may be beyond the limited resources of many private donor agencies. For crisis-management and environmental issues, developed countries possess the comparative advantage owing to their addressing similar difficulties at home. And peacekeeping and peacemaking might require the involvement of foreign governments or multilateral agencies with the capacity and legitimacy to act. If, as hypothesized here, donor governments will fund increasing amounts of international public good development assistance, there may be less resources for them to supply traditional aid, leaving a greater role for multilateral agencies and private agencies to give this form of development assistance. When donor countries give traditional development assistance through multilateral agencies, their money goes further if contributions are matched by other donors. The use of quotas or assessments by these agencies effectively lowers the price of giving a unit of aid-financed output. It is difficult to hypothesize whether total development assistance will increase in light of the need to supply these international public goods. A safer prediction is that the share of traditional development assistance in terms of overall development assistance will decrease, given cross-border exigencies and needs.

As mentioned earlier, clubs represent an alternative institutional arrangement for providing excludable public goods, funded through tolls that account for congestion costs. These clubs can consist of firms, nations, or other institutions. In the case of biotechnology and medicines, firms are anticipated to offer the club goods, thus raising equity concerns. Conventional aid may be required to permit some developing countries the means to participate in these clubs. This concern is aptly illustrated in the fight against the AIDS virus, for which drug combinations have been found to suppress the HIV virus. As a result, death rates from AIDS are down dramatically in the developed countries but are rising alarmingly throughout Africa where such medicines are not available. To circumvent equity concerns, developing countries' participation in some clubs can be funded through the common pool approach if these countries choose to put this participation in their development plans. For example, a recipient country may indicate financial resources needed to utilize INTELSAT or to purchase genetically engineered seeds. Clubs have much to recommend them since efficient outcomes, where resources go to their most valued use, can be achieved with little transaction costs. Members' utilization rates serve to reveal their tastes; members with stronger tastes for the club good pay more in total tolls.

The operation of a club hinges on two factors: excludability and a toll to charge for crowding. If a public good is excludable but does not display rivalry in the form of crowding, then the efficiency rationale for tolls can break down. Without crowding, there is no basis for charging a toll to adjust for the impact that one member's utilization has on the other members' well-being. Such excludable public goods can still be priced, but efficiency may be difficult to achieve, especially when a monopoly overcharges for the good.[43] This is the case when users' tastes differ and the supplier cannot tailor price to the diverse users' true taste for the shared public good.

Clubs also have the advantage of addressing recurrent costs problems that have plagued foreign-aid-assisted projects.[44] Because the toll is collected in each period and can also be tied to recurrent costs for maintenance of the good and other considerations, these recurrent costs are not a problem. Membership in these clubs can also give the developing countries a sense of ownership and participation. When multiple clubs form for related problems, some coordination among these clubs is necessary.

An appropriate institutional arrangement for supplying select *pure* public goods consists of regional networks or alliances that tie together nations with similar interests. One such successful network involves efforts by countries in West Africa to control river blindness.[45] Future networks could involve controlling malaria. These networks tend to form spontaneously when a public good problem significantly influences a well-defined group of countries. Efforts by such networks can be bolstered by development assistance either given to a participant's common pool request for funding to join the network or to the network directly. The primary participants in such networks are those countries most affected by the public good. This characterization of participation agrees with the subsidiarity principle presented in the next section. Networks to address global problems (e.g., HIV/AIDS) are often more difficult to form, because of the large number of heterogeneous countries involved. Nonetheless, regional branches may form first to coordinate localized efforts among countries in similar circumstances. A grander network may arise later to tie these branches together.

. . . .

SUBSIDIARITY AND INTERNATIONAL PUBLIC GOOD DEVELOPMENT ASSISTANCE

■　THERE IS ALSO A GEOGRAPHICAL QUESTION as to which countries or institutions should be involved with addressing a specific transnational public good problem. If the public good possesses a well-defined range of benefit spillovers, then ideally the principle of fiscal equivalence would dictate that the decision-making body's jurisdiction should coincide with the spillover region.[46] If, for example, a pest affects the crops of only four Latin American countries, then any institution (e.g., a partnership or alliance) that channels resources to fight this pest should include just these four countries. In principle, the organization of development assistance to address cross-border spillovers among a small set of developing countries will require the coming together of these developing countries and external donors willing to assist in solving the public good problem. The requisite group will differ by issue and spillover region. Groupings of affected countries may overlap with alternative public good concerns—one set being affected by vector-borne diseases, another set by security concerns, and yet another set by a pollutant. For issues that touch both developed and developing countries, such as infectious diseases, migrations, and labor standards, clearly all parties involved will have to participate in formulating and implementing allocative decisions and associated agreement on any compensatory transfer involved. For the direct production of international public goods like fundamental scientific or economic research, rich and poor countries both need to be involved in defining the direction of research, but implementation of the basic research can take place in the developed country or through institutions set up and financed by the donors.

The notion of fiscal equivalence suggests a mosaic of different structures to address the intersection between development assistance and transnational public good spillovers; ideally, a separate structure should be assigned to each international public good. This perfect coincidence between spillover and decision-making domains is conducive to an efficient allocation of these transnational public goods, since those people with the greatest stake in the decision can influence the provision level so that the associated benefits and costs are equated at the margin.

Although there are many institutions (e.g., World Health Organization, United Nations) associated with international public goods, there are many fewer such institutions than there are such goods. This follows because there are some important qualifications to fiscal equivalence. One such qualification involves *economies of scope* when the cost of providing two or more international public goods jointly by the same institution is cheaper than providing them by separate institutions. These economies of scope arise from savings derived from common costs when some inputs of the institution can serve more than one public good decision at the same time. If, for example, an existing international institution for some public good has infrastructure (e.g., administrative staff, communication network) with unused capacity, then use of this capacity to provide another public good may save sufficiently on cost to offset allocative losses from not matching the jurisdiction and the good's benefit range. The North Atlantic Treaty Organization (NATO), the

EU, and the United Nations provide a host of regional and global public goods to their members, and these public goods' spillover ranges do not always coincide. Even though economies of scope justify multiproduct institutions for which some noncoincidence occurs, there is a limit on how many public goods should be provided by the same institution. These economies of scope will eventually be exhausted or else be outweighed by either allocative inefficiencies from non-matching jurisdictions or adverse cross-linkage effects from using the same structure to address two or more distinct public goods. The latter would arise if the provision of one public good conflicted with the provision of another public good. For example, a development-promoting public good supplied by the U.N. Development Program may be at odds with another public good supplied by the U.N. Environmental Program, because different goals are being served by each of these U.N. organizations.

Another qualification can arise from economies of scale when the cost per unit in providing the public good decreases as more units are supplied to a larger region. It should be clear that economies of scale and scope suggest that a grouping together of different types of cases and functions would be cheaper than an individualized structure for each separate case. At the same time, there are myriad multilateral agencies specializing in regions and sectors, and it is unlikely that any grand consolidation of these will occur. Nevertheless, might there be a mapping from issues to organizations that serves as a first cut?

Consider the application of a *subsidiarity principle*.[47] A cross-border spillover should be handled by the agency whose geographical and sectoral mandate are closest to that issue, subject to the conditions that the agency possesses the capacity, or could be given the capacity to handle the issue, and that economies of scale and scope do not mandate a larger agency. The subsidiarity principle is an application of fiscal equivalence where the spillover range and institutional authority are matched as closely as possible among existing jurisdictions. Thus, for example, the first candidate to handle a cross-border transportation issue in West Africa might be the Economic Community of West African States (ECOWAS). If the capacity constraints or cost considerations of this subregional institution do not permit this issue to be addressed there, it should be raised to the next level of the AfDB, and only then, if the capacity is not present in the AfDB, should it be given to the World Bank to handle. In the medium term there should be a concerted effort to delegate authority and capacity to the lowest level possible subject to cost and efficiency considerations. In the case of Africa, this would argue for a significant strengthening of AfDB to deal with a range of cross-border issues in the region. Similar strengthening would apply to the IDB, which has already reflected the subsidiarity principle by successfully addressing numerous regional public good issues.

Cutting across the regional focus on local cross-border issues is the sector focus. The regional multilateral institution should take the lead in any local cross-border issue but should rely upon sectoral expertise from any multilateral institution that can supply it, including sectorally specialized agencies like the Food and Agriculture Organization (FAO). In the long run, it might be expected that such sectorally specialized agencies would provide much of the sectoral expertise. In the short run, however, agencies like the World Bank may be the only ones able to supply certain types of highly specialized sectoral expertise, or have the capacity to coordinate responses to localized cross-border problems. But with enough time, subsidiarity dictates regional and sectoral decentralization.

What is the appropriate institution for issues (e.g., financial contagion, drug trafficking, labor standards, and environmental practices) that cut across developed and developing countries? If institutions were tailored to each problem, there would be a plethora of institutions with overlapping memberships. One must, however, resist the urge to argue for some massive global authority; nations cherish their autonomy and show no proclivity to sacrificing it to a world body. At the global level, transaction costs are large and efforts to limit these costs by taking advantage of economies of scale and scope are necessary. Institutions that work best are those designed to deal with one or more related issues in a manner that preserves nations' autonomy over their general governance. Global institutions exist for many international cross-border concerns—e.g., the International Monetary Fund (IMF) for financial contagion, the World Trade Organization (WTO) for trade, the International Labor Organization (ILO) for labor standards, the United Nations for crisis management, the Universal Postal Union for mail, and the International Maritime Organization (IMO) for shipping. In the case of the IMO, nations sacrifice their autonomy over shipping practices, because it is in everyone's interest to have conventions on accident prevention, navigation, rescue at sea, innocent passage, pollution cleanup, and shipping practices.[48] Without the International Civil Aviation Organization, air corridors would be chaotic and prone to accidents. These international conventions are often extensions of domestic practices and, as such, abiding countries lose virtually none of their autonomy. For emerging-market economies, some of these conventions may not already exist domestically; nevertheless, it is in their interests to accept existing international practices to permit these countries' integration into the global community. A key instrument needed in these organizations is that of compensation for any short-run costs incurred by developing countries while adopting these standards.

Once again, a principle of subsidiarity applies to these more global public good problems. Subject to capacity constraints, the public good is best addressed by a specialized international agency rather than a more general structure like the World Bank or the United Nations. If the capacity does not exist in any of these specialist agencies or if economies of scope and scale are sufficient, then an agency like the World Bank can take responsibility initially until either this capacity is acquired or economies of scope and scale are no longer sufficiently significant. Over time as a general organization turns its attention to new problems, common costs may be better applied to these novel considerations, thereby curbing economies of scope for other considerations.

For those instances where development assistance can be given in the form of a public good produced by the donors and then made available to developing countries, it appears as though specialist arrangements will have to be made for each particular case, such as fundamental medical research on malaria and AIDS, or the development of new crop strains through genomic research. Current multilateral institutions do not as a rule have sufficient expertise to deliver on these, although they can serve as useful institutional structure for managing and channeling resources to such activities. An exception to this rule is fundamental research on the development process itself, where the multilaterals do seem to have a comparative advantage in terms of their capacity and their cross-country experience and activities. Synthesizing development experience is clearly a global public good, especially in an era when the detail of appropriate development strategies is no longer so clear and the world situation is so fluid. All multilateral institutions should begin to devote more resources to this task, with relevant sectoral or regional specialization as necessary.

Another factor that may favor eschewing the subsidiary principle and drawing on a multilateral institution has to do with the aggregation technology of public goods. For best-shot technologies, these larger institutions are better equipped to pool efforts to obtain a greater maximum contribution level. The alternative is to rely on the richest country to supply the good.

Even in a weakest-link scenario, multilateral institutions may be more suited to ensuring that all countries achieve an acceptable level of a global public good.

....

CONCLUSIONS

■ AID IN THE FORM OF PUBLIC GOODS with cross-border effects represents a new rationale for development assistance; however, international public good development assistance does not supplant the need for some traditional forms of assistance. Assistance in the form of international public goods represents a palatable kind of aid when donor countries benefit directly from this assistance. This acceptability may be reinforced in those instances where the donor provides the good itself, thus ensuring that resources are directed to their intended use. The variety of public goods in terms of their excludability, rivalry, and aggregation technology implies that simple principles that apply generally are not always possible to formulate. Nevertheless, we have reached some noteworthy conclusions:

- Common pool funding can be used to assist developing countries to provide national and international public goods if recipients favor these goods in their development programs. It is essential that traditional development assistance augments the capacity of developing countries to supply *and* to benefit from international public goods. This capacity building requires the acquisition of essential national public goods (e.g., technical know-how, education, secure and healthy environment).

- As the disparity between the richest and poorest countries widens, the richest countries may have to increase their provision of international public goods to developing countries. This is particularly true of those public goods that abide by best-shot and weakest-link aggregation technologies.

- The anticipated increase in "free-rider aid" may so tax direct country-provided assistance that multilateral and private agencies (including nongovernmental organizations) may have to assume an even greater role in providing traditional development assistance. It is suggested that, at times, donor countries are more suited to provide public goods, while multilateral and private agencies are better able to give conventional development assistance. Spillover benefits from these international public goods provide donor countries with the motivation to supply these public goods. To avoid the agency problem, a donor may want to supply some public goods directly.

- Income policies, in the form of tax-supported public goods and income transfers, are feasible when public good contributions are not perfectly substitutable among contributors. This lack of substitutability corresponds to when a summation aggregation technology does not apply or else joint products exist. In these cases, an increase in public good supply by one country does not necessarily crowd out the supply by another country.

- A subsidiarity principle is put forward that, subject to some provisos, cross-border concerns should be addressed by the institution whose geographical and sectoral mandate is nearest to the range of spillovers of the underlying public good. This essay does not call for new institution building, sufficient multilateral institutions exist to meet the challenge. The capacity of some regional institutions (e.g., IDB, AfDB) may, however, need to be increased.

- When exclusion can be practiced and crowding occurs, clubs offer an institutional arrangement based on user tolls for supplying international public goods efficiently while economizing on transaction costs. The use of clubs raises equity concerns when poorer countries are not able to afford the requisite toll. Common pool funding can be used to give developing countries the means to afford club goods that they voluntarily include in their development plan.

- Donor-specific benefits that are jointly produced with a public good can provide incentives to donors to contribute these goods to developing countries. Similarly, jointly produced recipient-specific benefits can give a sense of ownership to developing countries so that they assume recurring costs. The presence of joint products can make for more efficient outcomes.

- Whether to give the international public good directly or to transfer income depends, at times, on the aggregation technology of the good. For best-shot public goods, the developed country must provide the good at home and let its benefits spill over to the developing countries. For weakest-link public goods, a case can be made in the short term for providing the good directly to developing countries with weak capacity. In the longer run, however, developing countries must be assisted in acquiring the necessary capacity to supply these weakest-link goods themselves. Common pool assistance can help fund this capacity building. The best donor strategy for "summation" public goods depends on a number of considerations, including who is the most efficient producer and the range of spillovers.

In the next chapter, we turn to examine the relationship and interaction between two approaches to development assistance that have been proposed in this policy essay.

Notes

[1] The following contributions address some of these transnational externalities: Dieter Helm, ed., *Economic Policy towards the Environment* (Oxford: Blackwell, 1991); Inge Kaul, Isabelle Grunberg, and Marc A. Stern, eds., *Global Public Goods: International Cooperation in the Twenty-First Century* (New York: Oxford University Press, 1999); C. Ford Runge, "Common Property Resources in a Global Context," Center for International Food and Agricultural Policy Staff Paper no. P90-27 (Minneapolis, MN: University of Minnesota, 1990); Todd Sandler, *Global Challenges: An Approach to Environmental, Political, and Economic Problems* (Cambridge: Cambridge University Press, 1997); and Todd Sandler, "Global and Regional Public Goods: A Prognosis for Collective Action," *Fiscal Studies*, Vol. 19 (1998), pp. 221-47.

[2] On externalities and public goods, see Richard Cornes and Todd Sandler, *The Theory of Externalities, Public Goods, and Club Goods*, 2nd Ed. (Cambridge: Cambridge University Press, 1996).

[3] On the definition of a pure public good, see Paul A. Samuelson, "The Pure Theory of Public Expenditure," *Review of Economics and Statistics*, Vol. 36 (1954), pp. 387-9; Paul A. Samuelson, "A Diagrammatic Exposition of a Theory of Public Expenditure," *Review of Economics and Statistics*, Vol. 37 (1955), pp. 350-6; and Todd Sandler, *Collective Action: Theory and Applications* (Ann Arbor, MI: University of Michigan Press, 1992).

[4] See Congressional Budget Office, *The Role of Development Assistance in Development* (Washington, DC: Congressional Budget Office, 1997); and World Bank, *Assessing Aid: What Works, What Doesn't, and Why* (New York: Oxford University Press, 1998).

[5] See, for example, Richard Cornes, "Dyke Maintenance and Other Stories: Some Neglected Types of Public Goods," *Quarterly Journal of Economics*, Vol. 108 (1993), pp. 259-71; Cornes and Sandler, *The Theory of Externalities, Public Goods, and Club Goods*; and Jack Hirshleifer, "From Weakest-link to Best Shot: The Voluntary Provision of Public Goods," *Public Choice*, Vol. 41 (1983), pp. 371-86.

[6] On matching jurisdictional authority and the range of public good spillovers, see Albert Breton, "A Theory of Government Grants," *Canadian Journal of Economics and Political Science*, Vol. 31 (1965), pp. 147-57; Mancur Olson, "The Principle of 'Fiscal Equivalence': The Division of Responsibilities among Different Levels of Government," *American Economic*

Review Papers and Proceedings, Vol. 59 (1969), pp. 479-87; and Sandler, *Collective Action: Theory and Applications*.

[7] This health maintenance has clear transnational public good benefits. On this organization and its public good activities, see John F. Forbes, "International Cooperation in Public Health and the World Health Organization," in *The Theory and Structures of International Political Economy*, ed. Todd Sandler (Boulder, CO: Westview Press, 1980).

[8] Rajshri Jayaraman and Ravi Kanbur, "International Public Goods and the Case for Development Assistance," in *Global Public Goods: International Cooperation in the Twenty-First Century*, eds. Kaul, Grunberg, and Stern; Sandler, *Global Challenges: An Approach to Environmental, Political, and Economic Problems*; and Sandler, "Global and Regional Public Goods: A Prognosis for Collective Action."

[9] This required coincidence between the collective's borders and the range of benefit spillovers is known as fiscal equivalence. See Olson, "The Principle of 'Fiscal Equivalence': The Division of Responsibilities among Different Levels of Government."

[10] See Neil Bruce, *Public Finance and the American Economy* (Reading, MA: Addison Wesley Longman, Inc., 1998).

[11] There is an extensive literature on clubs which is surveyed by Cornes and Sandler, *The Theory of Externalities, Public Goods, and Club Goods*; Todd Sandler and John Tschirhart, "The Economic Theory of Clubs: An Evaluative Survey," *Journal of Economic Literature*, Vol. 18 (1980), pp. 1481-1521; and Todd Sandler and John Tschirhart, "Club Theory: Thirty Years Later," *Public Choice*, Vol. 93 (1997), pp. 335-55. Club theory was initially formulated in James M. Buchanan, "An Economic Theory of Clubs," *Economica*, Vol. 32 (1965), pp. 1-14; Charles M. Tiebout, "A Pure Theory of Local Expenditures," *Journal of Political Economy*, Vol. 64 (1956), pp. 416-24; and Jack Wiseman, "The Theory of Public Utility Price—An Empty Box," *Oxford Economic Papers*, Vol. 9 (1957), pp. 56-74.

[12] On INTELSAT, see Burton I. Edelson, "Global Satellite Communications," *Scientific American*, Vol. 236 (1977), pp. 58-73; INTELSAT, *INTELSAT in the '90s* (Washington, DC: INTELSAT, 1995); and Todd Sandler and William D. Schulze, "Outer Space: The New Market Frontier," *Economic Affairs*, Vol. 5 (1985), pp. 6-10.

[13] Congressional Budget Office, "Costs of Operation Desert Shield," Congressional Budget Office Staff Memorandum (Washington, DC: Congressional Budget Office, 1991); Congressional Budget Office, "Statement of Robert D. Reischauer, Director, Congressional Budget Office," Congressional Budget Office Testimony (Washington, DC: Congressional Budget Office, 1991); and Sandler, *Global Challenges: An Approach to Environment, Political and Economic Problems*.

[14] On joint products, see Richard Cornes and Todd Sandler, "Easy Riders, Joint Production, and Public Goods," *Economic Journal*, Vol. 94 (1984), pp. 580-98; and Richard Cornes and Todd Sandler, "The Comparative Static Properties of the Impure Public Model," *Journal of Public Economics*, Vol. 54 (1994), pp. 403-21.

[15] Roger Sedjo, "Property Rights, Genetic Resources, and Biotechnological Change," *Journal of Law and Economics*, Vol. 35 (1992), pp. 199-213.

[16] Nancy Birdsall, "Another Look at Population and Global Warming," Policy Research Working Papers, WPS 1020 (Washington, DC: World Bank, 1992).

[17] On charities and joint products, see James Andreoni, "Impure Altruism and Donations to Public Goods: A Theory of Warm-Glow Giving," *Economic Journal*, Vol. 100 (1990),

pp. 464-77; and John Posnett and Todd Sandler, "Joint Supply and the Finance of Charitable Activity," *Public Finance Quarterly*, Vol. 14 (1986), pp. 209-22.

[18] Cornes and Sandler, "The Comparative Static Properties of the Impure Public Good Model."

[19] The literature on neutrality includes Theodore C. Bergstrom, Lawrence Blume, and Hal. R. Varian, "On the Private Provision of Public Goods," *Journal of Public Economics*, Vol. 29 (1986), pp. 25-49; Cornes and Sandler, *The Theory of Externalities, Public Goods and Club Goods*; and Peter G. Warr, "The Private Provision of a Public Good is Independent of the Distribution of Income," *Economics Letters*, Vol. 13 (1983), pp. 207-11.

[20] Cornes, "Dyke Maintenance and Other Stories: Some Neglected Types of Public Goods."

[21] Richard Cornes and Todd Sandler, "Pareto-Improving Redistribution and Pure Public Goods," unpublished manuscript, (Ames, IA: Iowa State University, 1998).

[22] Jayaraman and Kanbur, "International Public Goods and the Case for Development Assistance."

[23] Nicholas van de Walle and Timothy A. Johnston, *Improving Aid to Africa*, Policy Essay No. 21 (Washington, DC: ODC, 1996).

[24] Hilde Sandnes, *Calculated Budgets for Airborne Acidifying Components in Europe, 1985, 1987, 1989, 1990, 1991, and 1992*, EMEP/MSC-W Report (Oslo: Norske Meterologiske Institutt, 1993); and James C. Murdoch, Todd Sandler, and Keith Sargent, "A Tale of Two Collectives: Sulphur versus Nitrogen Oxides Emission Reduction in Europe," *Economica*, Vol. 64 (1997), pp. 281-301.

[25] Higher labor standards are not always good, insofar as lower standards in developing countries can serve to "discipline" capital in developed countries. The most efficient set of standards lies somewhere between the lowest and highest, depending on a host of trade-offs.

[26] Another dimension for spillovers that could be added to Table 1 involves temporal considerations—say, between intragenerational and intergenerational spillovers. See Todd Sandler, "Intergenerational Public Goods: Strategies, Efficiency, and Institutions," in *Global Public Goods: International Cooperation in the Twenty-First Century*, eds. Kaul, Grunberg, and Stern; and Todd Sandler, "A Theory of Intergenerational Clubs," *Economic Inquiry*, Vol. 20 (1982), pp. 191-208.

[27] Each of the four aggregation technologies in Table 2 could be applied to each of the public good types in Table 1.

[28] On these aggregation technologies, see the references in note 5 and Simon Vicary, "Transfers and the Weakest-Link: An Extension of Hirshleifer's Analysis," *Journal of Public Economics*, Vol. 43 (1990), pp. 375-94. Also see Sandler, *Collective Action: Theory and Applications*; and Sandler, "Global and Regional Public Goods: A Prognosis for Collective Action."

[29] Desertification is discussed by Norman Myers, *Ultimate Security: The Environmental Basis of Political Stability* (New York: Norton, 1995).

[30] An exception would occur when a developing country, because of its location or interest, expends the greatest effort and is apt to be the one making the breakthrough.

[31] Cornes, "Dyke Maintenance and Other Stories: Some Neglected Types of Public Goods"; and Sandler, "Global and Regional Public Goods: A Prognosis for Collective Action."

[32] James Andreoni and Martin C. McGuire, "Identifying the Free Riders: A Simple Algorithm for Determining Who Will Contribute to a Public Good," *Journal of Public Economics*, Vol. 51 (1993), pp. 447-54.

[33] James Andreoni, "Privately Provided Public Goods in a Large Economy: The Limits to Altruism," *Journal of Public Economics*, Vol. 35 (1988), pp. 57-73; Cornes and Sandler, *The Theory of Externalities, Public Goods and Club Goods*; and Martin C. McGuire, "Group Size, Group Homogeneity, and the Aggregate Provision of a Pure Public Good under Cournot Behavior," *Public Choice*, Vol. 18 (1974), pp. 107-26.

[34] David T. Coe and Elhanan Helpman, "International R & D Spillovers," *European Economic Review*, Vol. 39 (1995), pp. 859-87.

[35] The effects of such attacks on FDI in Spain and Greece is empirically measured in Walter Enders and Todd Sandler, "Terrorism and Foreign Direct Investment in Spain and Greece," *Kyklos*, Vol. 49 (1996), pp. 331-52.

[36] On selective incentives, see Mancur Olson, *The Logic of Collective Action* (Cambridge, MA: Harvard University Press, 1965).

[37] Murdoch, Sandler, and Sargent, "A Tale of Two Collectives: Sulphur versus Nitrogen Oxides Emission Reduction in Europe."

[38] Todd Sandler and Keith Hartley, *The Political Economy of NATO: Past, Present, and into the 21st Century* (Cambridge: Cambridge University Press, 1999). Peacekeeping missions (e.g., Cambodia, Rwanda) are easier to characterize as international public goods than peace enforcement missions such as NATO's campaign in Kosovo begun in March 1999. For peace-keeping missions, opposing sides agree to the deployment of the peacekeeping forces.

[39] On the protocol's text under Article 5, see Richard E. Benedick, *Ozone Diplomacy* (Cambridge, MA: Harvard University Press, 1991); Scott A. Barrett, "On the Theory and Diplomacy of Environmental Treaty-Making," *Environmental and Resource Economics*, Vol. 11 (1998), pp. 317-33; Sandler, *Global Challenges: An Approach to Environmental, Political, and Economic Problems*; and United Nations Environmental Program, *Selected Multilateral Treaties in the Field of the Environment*, Vol. 2 (Cambridge, UK: Grotius Publications, 1991). Ozone-depleting substances contain either chlorine or bromine.

[40] United Nations Development Program, *Human Development Report 1992* (New York: Oxford University Press, 1992); and United Nations Development Program, *Human Development Report 1998* (New York: Oxford University Press, 1998).

[41] For a fuller discussion of these factors, see Sandler, "Global and Regional Goods: A Prognosis for Collective Action."

[42] On this fatigue see discussion in Chapter 2. Figures are provided in Congressional Budget Office, *The Role of Development Assistance in Development*.

[43] On excludable public goods, see Dagoburt L. Brito and William H. Oakland, "On the Monopolistic Provision of Excludable Public Goods," *American Economic Review*, Vol. 70 (1980), pp. 691-704; Michael E. Burns and Cliff Walsh, "Market Provision of Price-Excludable Public Goods: A General Analysis," *Journal of Political Economy*, Vol. 89 (1981), pp. 166-91; and Earl A. Thompson, "The Perfectly Competitive Production of Collective Goods," *Review of Economics and Statistics*, Vol. 50 (1968), pp. 1-12.

[44] van de Walle and Johnston, *Improving Aid to Africa*.

[45] We owe this example and insight to Marco Ferroni.

[46] Olson, "The Principle of 'Fiscal Equivalence': The Division of Responsibilities among Different Levels of Government."

[47] For a recent article on subsidiarity, see Sorpong Peou, "The Subsidiarity Model of Global Governance in the UN-Asean Context," *Global Governance*, Vol. 4 (1998), pp. 439-59.

[48] On such conventions see Todd Sandler, "Global Challenges and the Need for Supranational Infrastructure," unpublished manuscript (Ames, IA: Iowa State University, 1999); and Mark W. Zacher, *Governing Global Networks: International Regimes for Transportation and Communications* (Cambridge: Cambridge University Press, 1996).

Chapter 5
Further Thoughts
and Questions

This policy essay has argued that the future of development assistance has to be viewed in the context of three features of the current state of development thinking and policy. First, a broad consensus on appropriate development strategies, which appeared to be within reach as the Cold War ended, is no longer on the horizon. Essential differences of viewpoint have emerged on the pace and sequencing of liberalization, integration into the global economy, and on deeper social, structural, and institutional issues that need to be addressed but on which there is little agreement on how to proceed. Second, if there is any consensus, it is the recognition that development assistance has not been very effective in promoting development and poverty reduction, and that the practice of detailed and specific conditionality in the absence of country ownership has often failed. Third, new issues of cross-border spillovers and international public goods (IPGs) have come to the fore in a rapidly globalizing world and, by their very nature, international public goods are likely to be undersupplied in the global marketplace.

Within this context, we have explored two directions for the future of development assistance. First, on conventional country-specific development assistance, we have recommended a shift away from the highly intrusive aid mechanisms that have generally failed to date and proposed instead a "common pool" approach. Donors would not earmark their assistance for specific projects or programs but instead would pool their resources in support of a development program put forward by the recipient government. We have argued that this approach, which is the logical conclusion of initiatives currently under way, provides a way of reconciling different perspectives on development strategies, within the donor community and between donors and recipients, while promoting recipient ownership and donor coordination.

Second, cross-border issues and IPGs will and should become an integral part of the development assistance discourse. Such integration has already begun, but this policy essay has shown that simple and universal statements covering the rich range of IPGs are problematic. IPGs differ from one another along at least three dimensions—the geographical range of benefit spillovers, how individual actions aggregate to produce the overall supply of the IPG, and the extent to which potential beneficiaries of IPGs can be excluded or isolated. Each of these characteristics has significant implications for the design of schemes to address undersupply and, hence, for development assistance.

In particular, to address the differing geographical extent of the spillovers, we have proposed the principle of subsidiarity, in which cross-border issues are dealt with at the relevant level of decentralization through available institutions.

This essay is not of course a detailed blueprint on how the development assistance system should evolve. We have presented general arguments and a conceptual framework that now needs further operationalization. But there remain a number of questions and issues, even at the conceptual level. In particular, while we have discussed the common pool approach and international public goods as two important directions for the future of development assistance, these two issues have been for the most part treated independently. Are there connections and interactions, and perhaps tensions, between them? The answer is yes. We end this essay by highlighting five topics that need further work and discussion: 1) the measurement of development assistance in the presence of IPGs; 2) the tension between the common pool approach and the need for enforcing collective action in IPGs; 3) the problem of collective action in common pools; 4) implications for the volume and composition of conventional development assistance; and 5) the common pool approach, the subsidiarity principle, and the institutional architecture of development assistance.

. . . .

MEASURING DEVELOPMENT ASSISTANCE

■   CONSIDER THE PROBLEM OF INFECTIOUS DISEASES. There are at least two components to an international strategy to control the spread of such diseases. One is to develop vaccines for immunization. The second is actually to implement immunization by delivering the newly developed vaccines. The basic research needed for developing vaccines is frequently a "best-shot" technology, so that this will most likely be done in the richer (donor) country. Although this investment benefits the citizens of the donor country directly, it also has the potential to benefit the citizens of the poor country if the new research is made freely available and there is sufficient capacity in the latter to use the discovery. When a developed country's research spills over to a developing country, how much of this research spillover counts as development assistance? There are conceptual and empirical difficulties in answering this question. To the extent that the investment provides direct benefit to the citizens of the donor country, it might be best not to count it as assistance at all. On the other hand, to the extent that it does benefit the recipient country as a spillover, it might be counted as such. But the benefit of the spillover is not easy to conceptualize or calculate, since it depends not just on the vaccine research being made available, but on the immunization program being implemented in the poorer country. And of course a further conceptual problem is that to the extent that the immunization program is indeed implemented in the poor country, the citizens of the rich country will benefit, and we are back to the earlier argument that perhaps this should not be counted as "assistance" at all. Thus the introduction of IPGs raises some fundamental, and unanswered, questions on the measurement and classification of development assistance.

. . . .

IPGs AND THE COMMON POOL APPROACH

■   THE IMPLEMENTATION OF THE IMMUNIZATION PROGRAM discussed above has the characteristics of a "weakest-link" technology. It will be the country with the worst immunization program that will influence most, if not determine, the global spread of the disease. The "correction of under-supply" of this IPG therefore requires action in the poor country. We are then immediately faced with an agency problem. Given its poverty, the poor country will spend less than is globally optimal—and certainly less than the amount that donor countries would wish it to spend—on immunization. What to do? An immediate thought is conditionality—make funds available to the poor country on condition that they are incrementally spent on immunization. But this is open to all of the objections that led us to propose the common pool approach in the first place: such conditionality does not have a great record of success. Since different donors will be interested in different cross-border spillovers, they will each try to impose different conditionalities. And in any event, fungibility of resources puts restrictions on how much impact such conditionality can have. In the common pool framework, donors cannot earmark their resources for this or that specific project or program, and this guiding principle applies equally well to expenditures on IPGs. Hence, there is an incipient tension between the two perspectives we have advanced in this policy essay, and this needs further work and discussion.

Added to this are the tensions that arise when the country does not have the capacity to fully implement the common pool approach and when failure to supply the IPG represents a significant and immediate threat to donors and recipients. Projectized interventions may be appropriate in the short term under these conditions, but only with full inclusion of the country in design and implementation.

. . . .

COLLECTIVE ACTION
IN THE COMMON POOL

■ PUBLIC GOODS HAVE AN INHERENT FREE-RIDER PROBLEM which has been discussed in this essay. But the common pool approach has free-rider problems too. These are familiar in the conventional development assistance discourse and do not disappear just because we have a common pool approach. Dating back to the seminal work of Mancur Olson, "selective incentives" have been viewed as being able to attenuate the free-rider problem.[1] Thus, specific benefits going beyond the benefit of promoting development in the country—for example, constituency-specific benefits such as tied aid—can overcome the free-rider problem. But these constituency-specific forces were discussed at the start of this essay as part of the reason for the current problem in the aid delivery system, and they are what the common pool tries to get away from. Might the common pool not also reduce the incentives for development assistance? Possibly, but there are countervailing forces. First, greater aid effectiveness would appeal to constituencies in donor countries for whom no considerations other than development are important. Second, to the extent that greater prestige or similar donor-specific benefits are related to relative contributions to the common pool, this could set up a positive competition between donors. Third, the common pool may well lead to a sorting of donors so that a small number of donors will contribute the bulk of the resources for a given country, perhaps with a lead donor, thus reducing the free-rider problem.

In any event, the old issue of free riding in development assistance needs to be revisited in the context of the common pool approach.

· ·

IMPLICATIONS FOR VOLUME
AND COMPOSITION OF ASSISTANCE

■   IT IS NATURAL TO ASK WHAT OUR TWO DIRECTIONS for the future of development assistance imply for the volume and composition of development assistance. We have argued that, at least in the short run, the common pool approach might see a fall off in conventional aid flows. We have also argued that development assistance through contributions to the provision of "best-shot" IPGs might well be attractive to donors, because such assistance provides visible and direct benefits to the citizens of the donor country, while circumventing, to some extent, the agency problems of conventional assistance. Does this mean that there will be a shift in composition from conventional country-specific assistance? The answer to this is not entirely clear, because there are forces pulling in opposing directions. In the short run, IPGs' share of development assistance is expected to increase as many exigencies of a cross-border nature are addressed. If the effectiveness of aid improves as the result of the greater ownership and better donor coordination in the common pool approach, then the "aid fatigue" in donor countries might lift and country-specific aid flows could increase. Moreover, as we have seen, the supply of some IPGs can only be affected through actions at the country level, and this requires support of development through the common pool approach. It is, therefore, difficult to generalize regarding the long-run volume and composition of assistance as the result of common pools and IPGs; specific discussion of specific cases and countries is required.

· ·

SUBSIDIARITY, COMMON POOLS, AND
INSTITUTIONAL ARCHITECTURE

■   THE SUBSIDIARITY PRINCIPLE WE HAVE ADVANCED in this policy essay can in one sense be seen as a natural extension of the institutional design principles embodied in the common pool approach. Central to this approach is the diagnosis that attempts to resolve the donor-recipient agency problem through specific conditionality have typically failed. Although external funding can be modulated on the basis of an overall assessment of strategy, specific decisions, actions, and arrangements should be left to the country itself. Similarly, our subsidiarity principle says that in addressing cross-border spillovers, while funding can come from outside the geographical area of the spillover, specific decisions, actions, and arrangements should to the extent possible be left to the countries and regions affected by that spillover. Inherent in our argument is the position that the common pool approach and the subsidiarity principle do not necessarily require major redesign of the current institutional architecture for aid delivery. The current mosaic of overlapping institutions and mandates reflects not only different interests but genuinely different perspectives on development strategies. Since consensus on the latter is not in the offing, any "simplification" of the current system would surely be undone over time as different perspectives expressed themselves.

However, some institutional changes will be needed, and these need to be given careful consideration. The common pool approach will most likely mean reduction of the totality of staff in bilateral and multilateral institutions, and a specialization of staffs by institution to assess and evaluate different aspects of country programs for the donor community as a whole. The subsidiarity principle means a gradual shift of responsibility and staff from global to regional and local institutions for a range of cross-border and IPG issues. These conclusions raise some interesting but difficult questions: What, if any, will be the likely shifts in the share of conventional resource transfers going through various bilateral and multilateral institutions? Who should specialize in what areas of technical expertise? Over what time frame should the World Bank and U.N. agencies, for example, cede responsibility for Africa-specific cross-border issues to African institutions such as the African Development Bank (AfDB)? And what capacity needs to be built up in such regional institutions? What is the appropriate relationship between issue-specific institutions such as the World Health Organization and region-specific institutions such as the AfDB? While we do not see a radical change in the current institutional architecture as being realistic, answers to these questions may begin to sketch out the contours of the institutional landscape of development assistance in the decades to come.

. . . .

CONCLUSION

■ LOOKING SEPARATELY AT TWO CHALLENGES facing development assistance, this essay has concluded that the international community should move to implement a common pool approach to country-focused assistance and a nuanced approach to the use of development assistance for supplying international public goods. However, we have seen in this chapter that, in addition to the detailed operationalization required to implement these approaches, the *combination* of these approaches will require further conceptualization about their connections, interactions, and tensions. This chapter has outlined the issues that will need to be resolved in the years to come if these approaches are to be implemented and development assistance is to be made more effective. We hope that these issues will serve as a guide for further work and discussion, just as this essay can serve as a guide for future efforts to improve development assistance.

Note

[1] Mancur Olson, *The Logic of Collective Action* (Cambridge, MA: Harvard University Press, 1965)

About the Authors

RAVI KANBUR is the T.H. Lee Professor of World Affairs at Cornell University, where he teaches and conducts research on public economics and development economics. He is also Senior Advisor at the Overseas Development Council and a Fellow of the Centre for Economic Policy Research. From 1989 to 1997 he was on the staff of the World Bank, in various positions including Resident Representative in Ghana, Chief Economist of the Africa Region, and Principal Adviser to the Chief Economist of the World Bank. Before joining the World Bank he was Professor of Economics and Director of the Development Economics Research Centre at the University of Warwick, having previously taught at Oxford, Cambridge, Essex, and Princeton. He has published widely, in the leading economics journals as well as in policy fora, on a range of topics including risk, inequality, taxation, structural adjustment, debt relief, and development assistance.

KEVIN M. MORRISON is a Research Analyst at ODC, working on issues related to development assistance and international financial architecture. He has recently published work about the Asian financial crisis and the United Nations' role in development. Prior to joining ODC, he held positions at Yale University, the World Bank, and the Coca-Cola Company.

TODD SANDLER is a Distinguished Professor of Economics and Political Science, Iowa State University, Ames, Iowa, USA. His articles on a wide range of topics have appeared in such journals as the *American Economic Review, American Political Science Review, Quarterly Journal of Economics, Journal of Law and Economics, Journal of Public Economics*, and *Journal of Economic Theory*. In 1995-96, he co-edited (with Keith Hartley) the *Handbook of Defense Economics* (North-Holland, 1995), and co-authored (with Keith Hartley) *The Economics of Defense* (Cambridge University Press, 1995) and (with Richard Cornes) *The Theory of Externalities, Public Goods, and Club Goods*, 2nd Edition (Cambridge, 1996). His recent book, *Global Challenges* (Cambridge University, 1997), applies simple economic methods to study a range of problems including terrorism, acid rain, global warming, revolutions, and others. He is a recognized expert on terrorism, environmental economics, defense economics, and public economics. In 1999, he co-authored (with Keith Hartley) *The Political Economy of NATO: Past, Present, and into the 21st Century* (Cambridge, 1999), which examines both political and economic aspects of this enduring alliance. He has held positions at Arizona State University, University of Wyoming, and University of South Carolina. He has been a Visiting

Fellow at the Australian National University, University of Wisconsin, University of York, UK, University of Newcastle, Australia, Keele University, UK, and University of Aberdeen, Scotland. He currently serves on numerous editorial boards including *Journal of Public Economic Theory*, *Journal of Environmental Economics and Management*, *Defence and Peace Economics*, and *International Studies Quarterly*. During 1998-2000, he is a NATO Fellow.

About the ODC

The Overseas Development Council (ODC) is an independent, international policy research institution based in Washington, DC, that seeks to improve decision making on multilateral cooperation in order to promote more effective development and the better management of related global problems. Its program focuses on the interrelationship of globalization and development, and improved multilateral responses to these linked challenges.

To this end, ODC provides analysis, information, and evaluation of multilateral policies, actions, and institutions; develops innovative ideas and new policy proposals; and creates opportunities for decision makers and other interested parties to participate in discussions of critical global issues and decisions.

ODC is governed by an international Board of Directors of recognized and widely respected policy leaders on multilateral development and global issues. Peter D. Sutherland is its Chairman, and John W. Sewell is ODC's President.

ODC is a private, nonprofit organization, funded by foundations, governments, and private individuals.

O | D | C

OVERSEAS DEVELOPMENT COUNCIL
1875 CONNECTICUT AVENUE, NW
SUITE 1012
WASHINGTON, DC 20009
TEL. 202-234-8701
FAX 202-745-0067
http://www.odc.org

POLICY ESSAY NO. 25

ODC Board of Directors